MODERN NOVELISTS

General Editor: Norman Page

MODERN NOVELISTS

Published titles

SAUL BELLOW   Peter Hyland
ALBERT CAMUS   Philip Thody
IVY COMPTON-BURNETT   Kathy Justice Gentile
FYODOR DOSTOEVSKY   Peter Conradi
WILLIAM FAULKNER   David Dowling
GUSTAVE FLAUBERT   David Roe
E. M. FORSTER   Norman Page
ANDRE GIDE   David Walker
WILLIAM GOLDING   James Gindin
GRAHAM GREENE   Neil McEwan
CHRISTOPHER ISHERWOOD   Stephen Wade
HENRY JAMES   Alan Bellringer
JAMES JOYCE   Richard Brown
D. H. LAWRENCE   G. M. Hyde
ROSAMOND LEHMANN   Judy Simons
DORIS LESSING   Ruth Whittaker
MALCOLM LOWRY   Tony Bareham
THOMAS MANN   Martin Travers
GEORGE ORWELL   Valerie Meyers
ANTHONY POWELL   Neil McEwan
MARCEL PROUST   Philip Thody
BARBARA PYM   Michael Cotsell
JEAN-PAUL SARTRE   Philip Thody
SIX WOMEN NOVELISTS   Merryn Williams
MURIEL SPARK   Norman Page
JOHN UPDIKE   Judie Newman
EVELYN WAUGH   Jacqueline McDonnell
H. G. WELLS   Michael Draper
VIRGINIA WOOLF   Edward Bishop

Forthcoming titles

MARGARET ATWOOD   Coral Ann Howell
JOSEPH CONRAD   Owen Knowles
GEORGE ELIOT   Alan Bellringer
F. SCOTT FITZGERALD   John Whitley
JOHN FOWLES   James Acheson
ERNEST HEMINGWAY   Peter Messent
FRANZ KAFKA   Ronald Spiers and Beatrice Sandberg
NORMAN MAILER   Michael Glenday
V. S. NAIPAUL   Bruce King
PAUL SCOTT   G. K. Das
PATRICK WHITE   Mark Williams

MODERN NOVELISTS

SAUL BELLOW

Peter Hyland

St. Martin's Press   New York

First published in the United States of America in 1992

Printed in Hong Kong

ISBN 0–312–07598–7

Library of Congress Cataloging-in-Publication Data
Hyland, Peter.
Saul Bellow / Peter Hyland.
p.   cm.—(Modern novelists)
Includes bibliographical references (p.   ) and index.
ISBN 0–312–07598–7
1. Bellow, Saul—Criticism and interpretation.   I. Title.
II. Series.
PS3503.E4488Z7   1992
813'.52—dc20
                                      91–39681
                                          CIP

Contents

Every effort has been made to trace copyright-holders but if any
have been inadvertently overlooked the publishers will be pleased
to make the necessary arrangement at the first opportunity.

Note on References

It is the policy of this series to identify quotations from the texts by using chapter numbers. This raises problems with Saul Bellow's novels, some of which have unnumbered sections. To maintain uniformity, 'phantom' numbers have been assigned to the unnumbered divisions of the following novels: *Herzog, Humboldt's Gift, More Die of Heartbreak, A Theft* and *The Bellarosa Connection*. Quotations from *Dangling Man* are identified by the date of entry in Joseph's journal.

General Editor's Preface

The death of the novel has often been announced, and part of the secret of its obstinate vitality must be its capacity for growth, adaptation, self-renewal and self-transformation: like some vigorous organism in a speeded-up Darwinian ecosystem, it adapts itself quickly to a changing world. War and revolution, economic crisis and social change, radically new ideologies such as Marxism and Freudianism, have made this century unprecedented in human history in the speed and extent of change, but the novel has shown an extraordinary capacity to find new forms and techniques and to accommodate new ideas and conceptions of human nature and human experience, and even to take up new positions on the nature of fiction itself.

In the generations immediately preceding and following 1914, the novel underwent a radical redefinition of its nature and possibilities. The present series of monographs is devoted to the novelists who created the modern novel and to those who, in their turn, either continued and extended, or reacted against and rejected, the traditions established during that period of intense exploration and experiment. It includes a number of those who lived and wrote in the nineteenth century but whose innovative contribution to the art of fiction makes it impossible to ignore them in any account of the origins of the modern novel; it also includes the so-called 'modernists' and those who in the mid- and late twentieth century have emerged as outstanding practitioners of this genre. The scope is, inevitably, international; not only, in the migratory and exile-haunted world of our century, do writers refuse to heed national frontiers – 'English' literature lays claim to Conrad the Pole, Henry James the American, and Joyce the Irishman – but geniuses such as Flaubert, Dostoevsky and Kafka have had an influence on the fiction of many nations.

Each volume in the series is intended to provide an introduction to the fiction of the writer concerned, both for those approaching him or her for the first time and for those who are already familiar with some parts of the achievement in question and now wish to place it in the context of the total *oeuvre*. Although essential information relating to the writer's life and times is given, usually in an opening chapter, the approach is primarily critical and the emphasis is not upon 'background' or generalizations but upon close examination of important texts. Where an author is notably prolific, major texts have been made to convey, more summarily, a sense of the nature and quality of the author's work as a whole. Those who want to read further will find suggestions in the select bibliography included in each volume. Many novelists are, of course, not only novelists but also poets, essayists, biographers, dramatists, travel writers and so forth; many have practised shorter forms of fiction; and many have written letters or kept diaries that constitute a significant part of their literary output. A brief study cannot hope to deal with all these in detail, but where the shorter fiction and the non-fictional writings, public and private, have an important relationship to the novels, some space has been devoted to them.

                                                  NORMAN PAGE

1
Life and Career

When in 1976 Saul Bellow received the Nobel Prize for Literature the award marked the international recognition of a writing career that had already endured for thirty-five years. Yet it was only twelve years earlier, with the publication in 1964 of *Herzog*, that Bellow had begun to receive widespread popular attention in his own country, and this novel marked the confirmation of his status as 'major' American novelist, the inheritor of the place of Hemingway and Faulkner, both of whom had died during the three years prior to the appearance of *Herzog*. Bellow's earlier novels had brought him academic and critical acclaim as well as numerous literary prizes: *The Adventures of Augie March*, like *Herzog*, won the National Book Award, and he had received awards of various sorts from the National Institute of Arts and Letters and from the Guggenheim and Ford Foundations, as well as honorary doctorates from Northwestern University and Bard College. But the success of *Herzog* gave him a new prominence, for it marked him out as an author who was no longer the possession of a small, cultivated elite. *Herzog* remained on the best-seller lists for many weeks, and its popularity generated an interest in Bellow's earlier novels, which were reissued by their publishers with the recommendation that they were 'by the author of *Herzog*' or, more persuasively, 'by the celebrated author of *Herzog*'. Since then Bellow has won many other awards, including a further National Book Award (for *Mr. Sammler's Planet*) and a Pulitzer Prize (for *Humboldt's Gift*), making him the most honoured of contemporary American writers. His novels have continued to sell well.

The critical and academic acclaim that Bellow's writing has received is easy to understand. The publication in 1989 of two novellas, *A Theft* and *The Bellarosa Connection*, brought the canon of Bellow's fiction to a total of fourteen volumes (including two collections of short stories) written during a career spanning almost

1

fifty years.   In addition, Bellow has written a lengthy and highly
personal journalistic account of his experiences in Israel entitled *To
Jerusalem and Back*, a handful of plays, and a large number of
uncollected short stories, critical essays, and pieces of journalism
and social and political commentary.   It is a substantial and distinguished body of work, deeply serious, and marked by an intimate
awareness of the intellectual currents of the time and a persistent
engagement with the movement of contemporary history.   Why
Bellow should appeal to a popular audience and regularly make
the best-seller lists is more difficult to explain.   It is true that he is a
fine comic novelist, capable of effects ranging from the simple
farce of Henderson's adventures amongst the Arnewi to the subtle
ironies of Herzog's relationship with Valentine Gersbach, and that
he has created dozens of memorably eccentric secondary characters whose grotesque energies entitle them to be called 'Dickensian'.   He can also construct scenes of suspenseful excitement, like
the narrative of the iguana hunt in *The Adventures of Augie March*.
But he is an intellectually demanding writer who builds his novels
out of his own wide and eclectic reading, which encompasses vast
areas of the cultural history of Western civilization.   A single page
of a Bellow novel may contain references to Heine, Rousseau,
Robespierre, Kant, Fichte, Dryden and Pope, or to Ernst Junger,
Céline, Drieu La Rochelle, Brasillach, Ramon Fernandez and
Marguerite Duras.   And while an understanding of what Bellow is
about may not depend on a knowledge of the significance of these
figures, it is certainly enhanced by such a knowledge.
    It may well be that Bellow's eclecticism, the manner in which he
draws on a wide range of cultural fields and traditions not merely
as an intellectual basis for his fictions but as a means of examining
the polyglot nature of modern American experience, is the cause
of his popular reputation.   The American literary establishment,
for very good reasons, selected Bellow as the quintessential *American* writer of the post-war period.   In doing so they constituted him
as a cultural icon, and it is possible that many people buy his books
because he is Bellow, a man who, as bearer of the weight of the
Great American Tradition in fiction, yokes together the disparities
that make up contemporary American experience, and represents
American aspirations.   If this is true, he has become an object to be
possessed as much as a thinker to be read.   Bellow's popularity, that
is, may well be a product of the idea of his being 'the major
post-war American novelist'.

There is an irony as well as an inevitability about Bellow's inheritance of the mantle carried by Faulkner and Hemingway, since the two earlier novelists represented clear areas of traditional American experience. There may have been European influences on Faulkner's writing, but his creation of Yoknapatawpha County was an attempt to root America in its own history. And however far into Europe Hemingway's protagonists strayed they were still primarily *Americans*, struggling against an essentially American wilderness. Both novelists have a certain assurance of what it means to be American. Bellow represents a new generation with a different sense of what it is that constitutes American identity: the immigrant voice that articulates the experience of the displaced and the alienated. It seems peculiarly appropriate that the novelist who has been characterized by the critic Harold Bloom as 'By general critical agreement . . . the strongest American novelist of his generation'[1] should have begun by not being American at all.

Saul Bellow was, in fact, born in Canada. He was born Solomon Bellows in 1915 in Lachine, Quebec, the fourth child of Russian Jewish parents, Abraham Bellows and Liza Gordon Bellows. His parents had themselves hardly had time to become aware of what it meant to be Canadian, having immigrated from St Petersburg, Russia in 1913. Bellow was raised in the Rachel Market section of Montreal, one of the poorest areas of that city, and his early upbringing in the Montreal slums must have contributed much to the sense of cultural displacement and the intense desire for social or intellectual conquest that motivates so many of his protagonists, for the life lived there was essentially a continuation of the European experience from which the immigrants had fled. Bellow has written of this time: 'The Jewish slums of Montreal during my childhood, just after the First World War, were not too far removed from the ghettos of Poland and Russia. Life in such places of exile and suffering was anything but ordinary'.[2] But Bellow drew much from this 'ghetto' upbringing that was to feed his writing, for it tempered the sombre Jewish spirit of his orthodox religious education with the vernacular energies of Yiddish language and culture.

In 1924 the Bellow family moved to what must have seemed a much more expansive life in Chicago; at any rate Bellow felt at home there in a way that he clearly had not in Montreal. 'I grew up there and consider myself a Chicagoan out and out',[3] he has written, and although he has since then lived in many places

Chicago has remained his home. Bellow's early family life has
provided material for many of his novels, and he has spoken of the
ambivalence of his feelings about these years:

> I always had a great piety about my life. I always thought my life
> — I didn't think about it as my life when I was a kid — I thought
> it the most extraordinary, brilliant thing in the whole history of
> the universe that we should all be together. And there was so
> much unusable love that in the end it turned against itself and
> became a kind of chilliness, and for many years it stayed that
> way. . . . And then I realised that I was simply fooling myself.
> That it has really been a feast of love for me that I couldn't
> persuade the others to share.[4]

But the need to come to terms with this disappointed love has
occupied much of Bellow's artistic energy, and for so many of his
pained protagonists a part of the healing process is a return in
memory to childhood.

Bellow received his education in Chicago schools; he attended
Tuley High School, where he was the most precocious of a group
of boys who aspired to become famous writers, and who met
regularly to talk about what they had read and to read out their
own writings. In 1933 he entered the University of Chicago, where
he found his developing interest in literary and cultural subjects
made it difficult for him to work within the limitations of a
university course; as he put it some fifty years later:

> I was an enthusiastic (wildly excited) but erratic and contrary
> student. If I signed up for Economics 201, I was sure to spend all
> my time reading Ibsen and Shaw. Registering for a poetry
> course, I was soon bored by meters and stanzas, and shifted my
> attention to Kropotkin's *Memoirs of a Revolutionist* and Lenin's
> *What Is to Be Done?* My tastes and habits were those of a writer. I
> preferred to read poetry on my own without the benefit of
> lectures on the caesura.[5]

Bellow transferred to Northwestern University in 1935, and in
1937 he received from there an honours degree in sociology and
anthropology. In that same year he received a scholarship to
pursue graduate studies at the University of Wisconsin, but after a
few weeks he withdrew and returned to Chicago, marrying Anita
Goshkin at Christmas of that year.

Bellow was determined to become a writer, and for the next few years he lived on what might be called the literary fringe. In 1938 he was employed by the Works Progress Administration, at first to compile statistics about newspaper publishing, later to write biographical notes about Midwestern authors. Bellow himself has said he believes that the material generated by the WPA was never intended to be used, and that the WPA was set up mainly to give unemployed radical intellectuals like himself (Bellow had a youthful flirtation with Marxism) something to do. He taught at the Pestalozzi Teachers College in Chicago for a time, and between 1943 and 1946 he was briefly in the Maritime Service, and then was employed in the editorial department of the *Encyclopedia Britannica*, working on the 'Great Books' project (this was a project that undertook to compile all the seminal works that contributed to the development of Western culture). But he was also working on his own writing, and his first publication, a short story entitled 'Two Morning Monologues', appeared in *Partisan Review* in 1941; his first novel, *Dangling Man*, was published in 1944, followed by *The Victim* (1947).

Bellow's characteristic intermingling of incisive thought and imaginative wit, a power that can perhaps best be defined as 'intellectual charisma', was already apparent to his friends in these years, and is nicely caught in a brief memoir by the critic Alfred Kazin of his early impression of the novelist, whom he first encountered in the forties:

There was not the slightest verbal inflation in anything he said. Yet his observations were so direct and penetrating that they took on the elegance of achieved thought. When he considered something, his eyes slightly set as if studying its power to deceive him, one realized how formidable he was on topics generally exhausted by ideology or neglected by intellectuals too fine to consider them. Suddenly everything tiresomely grievous came alive in the focus of this man's unfamiliar imagination.[6]

Bellow's vast intellectual appetite and, it may be, his need for a sympathetic audience have kept him close to the academic world, and he has made a career as a teacher as well as a writer. He has taught English at a number of universities: in 1946 he was appointed to a position at the University of Minnesota in Minneapolis, and during the next few years he taught there and at New York University. In 1952 he was appointed Creative Writing

Fellow at Princeton. From there he returned to the University of
Minnesota, where he taught until 1959. His main affiliation is with
the University of Chicago, however. Since 1962 he has been
Professor of Letters and Literature there, and also a member of the
Committee on Social Thought, of which he was chairman from
1970 to 1976. The Committee on Social Thought is a body within
the university that offers flexible inter-disciplinary courses to a
small number of students and obviously must be highly congenial
to a man of Bellow's intellectual habits. Bellow himself always
seems a little wary of the academy but this university work has
allowed him to read and to talk, and has certainly fed his writing.

Bellow's first two novels were comparatively brief, disciplined
works, written in part after the manner of Flaubert, and expressing
a dark mood attributable, perhaps, to the grim time of their
conception: the post-Depression and wartime years in the case of
Dangling Man, and the immediate post-war years in the case of *The
Victim*. In 1948, however, Bellow was awarded a Guggenheim
Fellowship which allowed him to travel extensively in Europe,
especially in France, Italy and Austria. He lived for some time in
Paris, and began work on *The Adventures of Augie March*. According
to Bellow the book was written mainly in trains and in cafes.
Perhaps the relaxation of this time had something to do with the
quite different manner of *Augie March*: expansive and optimistic,
the novel introduced a sprawling form and a delight in rhetoric
that were to become Bellow's characteristic mode. Bellow returned
to the United States, and lived for most of the fifties in New York.
He became a member of the circle of Jewish intellectuals associated
with the journal *Partisan Review*, and began his influential
friendship with the poet and critic Delmore Schwartz. *The Adventures of Augie March* was published in 1953, and received the
National Book Award that year. He published two more novels
during that decade: *Seize the Day* (1956) and *Henderson the Rain King*
(1959). *Seize the Day* is, strange to say, the only one of Bellow's
novels so far to have been filmed: released in 1986, the film was
directed by Fielder Cook and starred Robin Williams. It is remarkably faithful to the book.

There is not much to be said about Bellow's personal life during
these years, or, indeed, at any time, for in spite of his increasing
public eminence he has always been an essentially private man,
anxious to be in full control of what he reveals about himself. In the
late fifties the writer Mark Harris conceived the idea of writing a

biography of Bellow and for almost twenty years he persevered in his attempts to persuade Bellow to allow him to be his official biographer. He never did get Bellow's permission, however, because of the novelist's reluctance to be pinned down, and he produced no biography, though he did write a book about his attempts to produce one, in which, at the very end, he quotes Bellow on such intrusions into his privacy: 'The less I see about my life the better.'[7] The most that need be said here is that his personal life was not easy. In 1956 he married Alexandra Tschacbasov, having divorced his first wife; this marriage also ended in divorce, and he married Susan Glassman in 1961. He has a son by each of these wives. Bellow's sour experience of the aftermath of divorce, and especially of lawyers and the painful conflict over alimony, provided rich comic material for some of the later novels, most notably for *Herzog*.

Bellow returned permanently to Chicago in 1962. It would be difficult to overestimate the importance for Bellow's writing of that great Midwestern city and his relationship to it. Chicago is the embodiment of American material aspirations; it developed through the first decades of the present century as a place where money could be made by the displaced masses flocking into it, and more than any other major American city it derived its quality from immigrant groups, its raw energy from the crude, often brutal desires of men who were 'making it', moving from poverty to wealth, from vulgarity to culture. The city had already provided the material out of which writers like Theodore Dreiser and James T. Farrell had produced novels about the cruelty, aimlessness and boredom of urban life: solid, naturalist works that had no small influence on Bellow's own fiction. Thematically, Chicago provides the battleground on which Bellow's protagonists struggle to find or hold on to their identity, to identify some spiritual value within the vast metropolitan clutter of objects and people that constantly threatens to crush them. But this clutter influences Bellow's style too, with its lists of *things* that try to find order in randomness, like this passage from *Dangling Man*: 'ranges of poor dwellings, warehouses, billboards, culverts, electric signs blankly burning, parked cars and moving cars, and the occasional bare plan of a tree'. Chicago is the American melting pot, and Bellow's own life there, uniting the slum and the academy, accounts for the fact that in his novels the American voice he reproduces is both metropolitan and cosmopolitan. The characteristic narrative voice in a Bellow novel

articulates an urban experience that is interpreted through an
artistic vision that draws on a vast European spiritual tradition as
well as on the blood and dirt of the stockyards; it is a voice that is
both literate and street-wise. Bellow works hard to keep the voice
authentic, as he indicated in a 1973 interview: 'Now I do divert
myself in Chicago. I leave the university fortress to go to play
squash twice a week downtown with businessmen, stockbrokers,
lawyers, psychologists, builders, real estate people, and a sprinkling
of underworld characters and old school friends who are not
particularly aware of the fact that I am a writer.'[8]

Herzog was published in 1964; its immense popular success took
Bellow by surprise. He expected it to achieve the comparative
obscurity of 8000 copies, but it remained on the *Publishers Weekly*
best-seller list for 43 weeks, 25 of them as number one, and won
numerous awards apart from the prestigious National Book Award
and the International Literature Prize. It also conferred upon him
a status as public figure that he had not previously enjoyed – and
perhaps 'enjoyed' is an ill-chosen word here, for Bellow has
frequently shown his disquiet about the ways in which popularity
and the concern to please an audience or the willingness of a writer
to submerge his personal vision and blind himself to the ugliness all
around him might erode his independence and integrity of judgement. The risks entailed in such a loss are considered in his
acceptance speech for the National Book Award:

> it is the task of artists and critics in every generation to look with
> their own eyes. Perhaps they will see even worse evils, but they
> will at least be seeing them for themselves. They will not, they
> cannot permit themselves, generation after generation, to hold
> views they have not examined for themselves. By such willful
> blindness we lose the right to call ourselves artists; we have
> accepted what we ourselves condemn – narrow specialization,
> professionalism, and snobbery, and the formation of a caste.[9]

Bellow is insisting on the artist's right – a right that is, in fact, a duty
– to dissent from the complacency of consensus.

In the mid-sixties Bellow digressed briefly from fiction into
theatre. His play *The Wrecker* was televised in 1964, and in the same
year his only full-length play *The Last Analysis* opened at the Belasco
Theatre, New York City, and closed after 28 days. *The Last Analysis*
is an interesting piece of work, a blackly satirical farce that has a
great deal of potential, but it was written by a man accustomed to

writing expansive novels, and does not have the coherence a theatre audience demands. The play as Bellow re-wrote it for publication reads rather well, but Bellow was embittered by the experience, as his reference to 'the cold and peevish first-night audience, the judgments of the critics'[10] in a prefatory note to the printed edition indicates. In the following year he made a further attempt to move into the theatre: three short plays, 'Out from Under', 'Orange Soufflé' and 'A Wen', were staged privately off-Broadway. In 1966 they were staged in London under the title *The Bellow Plays*, and in Glasgow, New York and Spoleto, Italy with the title *Under the Weather*. They did not generate much interest, and their lack of success discouraged Bellow from further attempts at writing for the theatre.

Bellow was always an incisive commentator on the American social, cultural and political scene; the range of characters and locations in his collection *Mosby's Memoirs and Other Stories* (1968) demonstrates this. But his preoccupations extended increasingly to the world at large. He travelled widely in Europe and the Middle East, and in 1967 he reported on the Six-Day War for *Newsday* magazine. What he saw in Israel may have stirred his perennial concern with the suffering of the Jewish people; at any rate, the evil of the Holocaust pervades his next novel, *Mr. Sammler's Planet* (1970), more than any of his earlier works. There has been much critical disagreement about this novel, but it brought him his third National Book Award.

In 1974 Bellow was married for the fourth time, to Alexandra Ionescu Tulcea, a Rumanian-born mathematician who would renew Bellow's connections with Eastern Europe and revive his concerns about modern Communism. In the following year he travelled with her to Israel, where they stayed for some months. In that year he also published *Humboldt's Gift*, for which he received the Pulitzer Prize. This is the novel that most rivals *Herzog* as Bellow's masterpiece; its panorama of Chicago life, both high and low, creates a melting pot in which writers, criminals, lawyers and businessmen are brought together in a brilliantly levelling manner. Much of the pain of his own past emerges in this book only to be transformed into comedy: his relationship with the precocious but doomed poet Delmore Schwartz, his wounding marriages, his failures as editor (in the early sixties he had co-edited a literary journal, *The Noble Savage*, which survived for only a couple of years) and as dramatist.

But failure for Bellow was increasingly a thing of the past. In the following year he received the Nobel Prize for Literature in recognition of his perpetuation of enduring values. In his novels, according to the Nobel committee, he portrays 'a man who keeps on trying to find a foothold during his wanderings in a tottering world, one who can never relinquish his faith that the value of life depends on dignity, not its success, and that truth must triumph at last'.[11] The emphasis here is on uplift rather than art. While Bellow was happy to be awarded the prize, he was quite concerned about its implications. He noted that earlier American writers who had received it had gone into a decline, and he was afraid that the complacency it might generate could cut him off from the sources of his creative energy. This suspicion of the destructive possibilities of celebrity is reflected in an interview given shortly after his receipt of the Prize: 'The worst fear I have as a writer is that of losing my feeling for the common life, which is, as every good writer knows, or should know, anything but common. To think of oneself as a Nobel Prize winner is finally to think of oneself as an enameled figure in a China cabinet, and I don't intend to find myself in a China cabinet.'[12]

Bellow did not completely avoid the dangers inherent in being a public figure, however; in that same year he published his book *To Jerusalem and Back: A Personal Account*, which is a journal of his visit of the previous year. In it he describes his encounters with a wide range of characters, from Teddy Kollek, Mayor of Jerusalem, to Moshe the masseur, a Montreal Jew like Bellow himelf. Not surprisingly, a main concern is Israel's struggle to survive, and the book gives eloquent expression to that concern; but it is also, as Bellow insists, a personal account, a reassessment of his own Jewish past and of his sense of being in exile. It is, furthermore, a saddened response to what Bellow calls 'the eagerness to kill for political ends'. But however hard he tries, Bellow cannot put events in the Middle East into a perspective that is in any way sympathetic to the Arab cause. Inevitably he was attacked for his pro-Israeli stance, most notably by the Jewish-American intellectual Noam Chomsky, who accused him of presenting a simplistic analysis of political events that amounts to propaganda for the Zionist cause.[13] The fate of Israel remained a major preoccupation for Bellow, however, and in 1979 he once again reported for *Newsday* magazine, this time on the signing in Washington of a peace treaty by Sadat, Carter and Begin.

It is not only for what is perceived as a reactionary political stance that Bellow has been attacked. In recent years, in articles and interviews, he has become increasingly vocal as a commentator on what he sees as a slide towards anarchy in the decline of literacy and culture in the Western world, which he associates with the loss of a sense of what it means to be a human being. Despite his own professional attachment to the University of Chicago, he has indicated that he believes that Western education is failing to provide for the needs of the soul, and the strength of his conviction is indicated by his willingness to provide a foreword to the 1987 book *The Closing of the American Mind* by the neoconservative social philosopher Allan Bloom, a book which loudly calls attention to the diminishing intellectual horizons of the current 'enlightened' age.

These are ideas that are fundamental to Bellow's novels, however, and in spite of his incursions into what may be considered to be cultural or political journalism, Bellow has remained a writer of fiction, and has refused to go into retirement; indeed, in the eighties he has been, if anything, more productive than ever before, producing five volumes of fiction. In the years following his receipt of the Nobel Prize Bellow often seemed increasingly waspish, his engagement with history inclining him toward a deeper pessimism. In *The Dean's December* (1982) he is more concerned than in earlier novels with public matters; he presents a bleak picture of life under Communist rule, but its accompanying picture of American urban decay is hardly less bleak. The novel is barely relieved by the comic vision that distinguishes Bellow's most characteristic work, and when it appeared many critics saw in it signs of fatigue. But since *The Dean's December* Bellow has been uncharacteristically prolific, following on in 1984 with a collection of short stories entitled *Him with His Foot in His Mouth*, and in 1987 with the novel *More Die of Heartbreak*, which is closer to the mode of *Herzog* and *Humboldt's Gift*. In 1989 he published two novellas, *A Theft* and *The Bellarosa Connection*.

In the current year (1991) he is still living and writing in Chicago, having recently married his fifth wife, Janice Friedman. He is working on another novella, and still resisting the efforts of biographers to pin down his life, though a volume by Ruth Miller, an acquaintance of Bellow's for many years, is due to appear shortly, and James Atlas is working on what he intends will be the definitive book on Bellow's life. Bellow himself is acutely aware of the sense of finality that a biography gives to the career of a living writer, and so explains his reluctance to help these biographers: 'I don't think the game is over till it's over. So I do drag my feet a bit, but it's not out of ill will. My attitude is, I'm busy, let me be. I'm still struggling, battling, fighting, whatever you want to call it, to get it right. I haven't hung up my gloves yet'.[14] And that surely is not the final word.

2
Novels of the Forties

Looked at in retrospect the canon of Bellow's fiction exhibits a remarkable degree of uniformity, but it would be presumptuous to attempt to render the literary output of a fifty-year career down to a few simple formulae; from relatively limited beginnings Bellow has developed a rich and complex body of work of extensive intellectual scope, which to a degree unequalled amongst contemporary writers has attracted the attention of academic critics and scholars. Books have been written on his humanism, his nihilism, his comic vision, his debt to Jewish tradition, his treatment of history, his position in relation to modernism. Clearly, a study of the dimensions of the current one cannot hope to do justice to this profusion. Still, some general observations can be made about Bellow's work.

His novels are constantly and dynamically engaged with contemporary history. With few exceptions, his fictions take place at the historical moment at which they were written, and taken as a body his work reflects the flux of ideas and the major political and cultural tensions that have affected the Western world in the decades since World War II (Bellow's America is metonymic of the West, representing, in effect, the modern world). In one sense it could be said that the central tension that creates history is between high idealism and mundane reality, and that a key manifestation of this in Bellow's novels is the American city as represented by Chicago (there are other cities in Bellow's fiction but the pressure they exert on his protagonists is the same: consider Asa Leventhal's New York or Kenneth Trachtenberg's anonymous Midwestern city). This city, defined by its exciting, crushing material weight and inhabited by mass man, its luxurious skyscrapers overlooking urban devastation, provides Bellow with a powerful metaphor for the present historical moment, and one of the great strengths of his prose is its ability to suggest the texture of urban experience. For

Naturalist writers like Dreiser, who preceded Bellow in writing about Chicago, this historical weight was deterministic, defining identity. Bellow resists this view of individual definition, however, as he shows in his account of his own response to Chicago:

> The commonest teaching of the civilized world in our time can be stated simply: 'Tell me where you come from and I will tell you what you are.' There was not a chance in the world that Chicago, with the agreement of my eagerly Americanizing extended family, would make me in its image.[15]

Like Bellow, his protagonists are all involved in a struggle to avoid being taken over by this determinism. But for them to be able to define themselves apart from history they have to be able to understand it. As Kenneth Trachtenberg puts it in the opening chapter of *More Die of Heartbreak*:

> unless your thinking is deduced from a correct conception of history, unless you live in your time, thinking will only confuse you – it will drive you nuts. The terrible result of hyperactive but unfocused consciousness is a cause of our decline.   (36)

For the Bellow protagonist, to assert himself as an individual, to know his own identity, is to understand history, and this is to understand ideas, to understand the theories by which men have lived that have led to things being as they are.

This means that the Bellow hero (especially in the novels from *Herzog* onwards) is faced with a formidable task: to assert his distinct identity he must sort through the vast confusion of ideas and separate the valuable from the bogus. The bad ideas, the false conceptions that caused the decline Kenneth talks about are plentiful, and most of Bellow's heroes are tempted by eloquent proponents of theories that provide easy answers for mass men, by what the novels call 'Machiavellians', 'sharpies' and 'shrewdies', or, most memorably, 'reality instructors'. To avoid falling into the 'reality' trap they have to distance themselves from false theories and this accounts for the vast weight of abstract and often obscure ideas that they carry around, the compulsive intellectual activity that makes, for example, Herzog analyse what it means to be modern urban man while he is waiting for Ramona to appear in a G-string.

With only a couple of exceptions (Eugene Henderson and Albert Corde) the Bellow hero is Jewish, culturally displaced and feeling himself marginalized within American society (the fashionable word when Bellow began writing was 'alienated'). Especially in the later novels he tends to be an intellectual, a scholarly or literary figure, sometimes a teacher or a journalist – a figure like Bellow himself and, not infrequently, given to pontificating on the kinds of cultural and political question that Bellow himself talks about in lectures and interviews. Since Bellow has always been willing to mine his own experience for material for his novels (for the young Augie March's Chicago home, for example, or Herzog's Montreal childhood or his dealings with ex-wives and divorce lawyers) his protagonists have frequently been taken as mouthpieces for Bellow's own views (an assumption that is encouraged by the fact that the protagonist is often the narrator of his own story and always its central consciousness), and the author has been criticized for a failure to distance himself from his creation. Bellow himself has dealt most gracefully with this tendency to identify him with his characters: 'I would have to suffer from dissociation of personality to be all these people in the books. I can't possibly be all of them. I lend a character, out of pure friendship, whatever he needs, that's all'.[16] Bellow is being rather disingenuous here, of course, and there is certainly more of Bellow in his novels than this suggests; but as we shall see, the ironic mode of much of his writing, coupled with the clear presence of Bellow's voice in his work, leaves open the constant possibility of ambiguity of meaning. This ambiguity has often been seen as an artistic weakness, but it is, I think, intentional, and an indication of Bellow's refusal to supply clear and easy answers to the complex problems he presents.

Bellow's two earliest novels have much in common. *Dangling Man* and *The Victim* are sparely written books, claustrophobic in their effect, controlled and precise in style, sombre in tone. Their narrative voice is distant from the exuberant, expansive voice that is heard in the most characteristic of Bellow's works. In both of them the protagonist is dislocated from his normal life and subjected to a testing situation that exerts pressure on his sense of who or what he is, and that leaves the reader unsure of whether or not the test has been survived. The essential bleakness that the two books share can be accounted for in part by the fact that they were written under the immediate shadow of World War II, but they seem to reflect a more general unease about the insecurity and fragmentation of modern urban life. Critics have sometimes dismissed these books as minor works in Bellow's canon; to Harold Bloom, for example, they 'seem now to be period pieces'.[17] Bellow himself has noted how their formal rigour suggested aesthetic limitation: 'These books, though useful, did not give me a form in which I was comfortable'.[18] Certainly the pattern of Bellow's career suggests that his skills are better demonstrated by the more expansive forms of such novels as *The Adventures of Augie March, Herzog* and *Humboldt's Gift*. Nevertheless, these two novels are unmistakeably Bellow's: they may lack the intellectual complexity, as well as the more overt comedy, of the later novels, but the *kind* of crisis and self-examination that their protagonists, Joseph and Leventhal, undergo clearly makes them forerunners of the later Bellow heroes.

  Dangling Man was not Bellow's first published fiction; a short story entitled 'Two Morning Monologues' had appeared in the journal *Partisan Review* in 1941. The first of the two monologues is that of a young man named Mandelbaum who is out of work and waiting to be drafted into the armed forces; he is passive and introspective, and in some senses a prototype for Joseph in *Dangling Man*. It is paired with the monologue of an unnamed gambler, a man who recognizes that the system in which he is involved is bad, but who believes that he can control it, that he can find 'a way through the cracks'. Both men, the passive and the active, are failures, and the story shows them both as being responsible for their own failure. The monologues are juxtaposed without comment, leaving the working out of their implications to the reader. Mandelbaum is the prototype not just for Joseph, however, but for many of Bellow's heroes, and while it would be a gross over-simplification to claim that all his fiction is based on a juxtaposition similar to this one, it is certainly true that many of his protagonists are sensitive and introspective figures like Mandelbaum, whose vision of the world is interrogated by 'reality instructors' or 'Machiavellians' – characters who believe, like the gambler, that the world can be controlled.

  Whether or not *Dangling Man* is now only a period piece, as Bloom claims, is debatable (though the term itself is ill-chosen, since all literary works are primarily products of their own time), but when it first appeared in 1944 its significance as a war novel of a new kind, a document about the effects of the war on the intellectual, the war's ability to make casualties out of noncombatants, to alienate and marginalize, was immediately noted in literary circles. As the critic Edmund Wilson saw it, the book was 'one of the most honest pieces of testimony on the psychology of a whole generation who have grown up during the war', while the poet Delmore Schwartz wrote: 'Here, for the first time I think, the experience of a new generation has been seized and recorded'.[19] *Dangling Man* remains a book that has to be taken seriously, both as a novel of its time and as a stage in Bellow's career. It shows him as a writer who profits from a wide and eclectic variety of sources. Apart from the formal influence of Flaubert, critics and scholars have traced many other influences from European writers concerned with social and personal disintegration, most notably the work of Dostoevsky, Kafka, Sartre and Camus. Joseph has clear affinities with the protagonist of Dostoevsky's *Notes from Underground*, a frustrated intellectual who is filled with a loathing both of himself and of the world, but Joseph's concern with the limitations of freedom and the quest for identity allies him also to the alienated existentialist heroes of such fictions as Sartre's *Nausea* and Camus's *The Stranger*, and he has much in common with the victimized and isolated figures of Kafka's novels. Bellow also drew from his own Jewish heritage, from a history of persecution and a tradition of writing that obstinately found comedy within the nightmare that it explored. Bellow himself, in his introduction to *Great Jewish Short Stories*, defined what he considered to be the essential characteristic of this body of Jewish writing: 'laughter and trembling are so curiously mingled that it is not easy to determine the relations of the two'.[20]

While the European influences must be acknowledged, Bellow was concerned to stake out a position for himself in the American literary tradition, one that embraced feeling and sensitivity and set itself in opposition to the then-current 'hard-boiled' school of writing associated with Ernest Hemingway. This is what we find in the novel's opening paragraph, Joseph's statement of his separation from the times:

For this is an era of hardboiled-dom. Today, the code of the athlete, of the tough boy – an American inheritance, I believe, from the English gentleman – that curious mixture of striving, asceticism, and rigor, the origins of which some trace back to Alexander the Great – is stronger than ever. Do you have feelings? There are correct and incorrect ways of indicating them. Do you have an inner life? It is nobody's business but your own. Do you have emotions? Strangle them.

Hemingway's protagonists are fighters, men who oppose the terrors of nothingness and make themselves into heroes by struggling to impose themselves upon the frontiers of natural wilderness, who express their heroism through displays of physical courage that put them in constant confrontation with death. There is something undeniably adolescent about this view of heroism, and Bellow pits his heroes against a wilderness of an entirely different kind. For Bellow, the struggle is to salvage something of the self under the crushing pressures of urban life, of modern materialism and self-indulgence.

Dangling Man is written in the form of a journal, covering a period of about four months from 15 December 1942 to 9 April 1943. The author of the journal, identified simply as 'Joseph', has quit his job because he is expecting to be drafted into the army. Joseph's journal, which is Bellow's novel, gives an account of his social, intellectual and spiritual experience, as he 'dangles' in personal disorder between the ordered worlds of work, which he has quit, and the army, which he is waiting to join. This period ought to be a time of freedom, but Joseph does not know how to use it. He sees himself as dislocated from his own past by the events of history, and, left to his own resources, he gradually separates himself from the external world: he begins to depend completely upon what goes on in his own mind, and so he ceases to read, and he becomes alienated from his friends, his brother and family, his mistress, and even his wife. This casting-off of relationships forces him to turn inwards until he can talk only to himself: he invents an alter-ego which he calls the 'Spirit of Alternatives', but he is defeated even by this version of himself when he is forced to face the possibility that he may not have a separate destiny. The novel ends with Joseph, unable to bear the burden of his 'freedom', asking the draft board to expedite his induction into 'regular hours' and 'regimentation'.

Early in *Dangling Man*, in his entry for 17 December, Joseph surveys the Chicago landscape from the window of his slum rooming house. The wrecked cityscape he sees is, in effect, the outward representation of history, and he considers the account of the modern human spirit that is implied by the random ugliness of the scene:

Where was there a particle of what, elsewhere, or in the past, had spoken in man's favor? There could be no doubt that these billboards, streets, tracks, houses, ugly and blind, were related to interior life. And yet, I told myself, there had to be a doubt. There were human lives organized around these ways and houses, and that they, the houses, say, were the analogue, that what men created they also were, through some transcendent means, I could not bring myself to concede. There must be a difference, a quality that eluded me, somehow, a difference between things and persons and even between acts and persons. Otherwise the people who lived there were actually a reflection of the things they lived among.

Joseph can find no beauty in the scene and is forced to conclude that its barrenness is a reflection of the human spirit that created it, but at the same time his own spirit struggles against any such conclusion, and sends him on a quest for something that he can set up counter to this ugliness. 'How should a good man live; what ought he to do?' he asks himself (22 December), and these are questions asked in one way or another in all of Bellow's novels. The answers, if there are any, involve a search within the self, an assertion of an identity that endures in spite of all that the world can do to annihilate it: 'to know what we are and what we are for, to know our purpose, to seek grace' (22 February).

Joseph's search for grace is presented as another monologue, a conversation he carries on with himself in the journal that he writes, as he says, because he has become isolated, spending ten hours a day alone in a single room. He has stopped seeing his friends, and his only regular human contact is his wife Iva, but he has little communication even with her. His neighbours irritate and dispirit him, and on the occasions when he leaves his room he tries to avoid meeting anyone he knows. His journal details his daily experiences, but it also recounts events in the past that he thinks of as notable stages in his progress towards his current alienated state, and it presents his attempts at self-analysis and at understanding the significance of his experiences. The result of this analysis is a paradox that Joseph never succeeds in resolving. He cannot answer the questions he asks about the relation of his interior life to the external world, nor does he know where to locate the blame for the breach between himself and the world that he is unable to bridge. For how is the grace he seeks to be found? As Joseph sees only too clearly, 'goodness is achieved not in a vacuum, but in the company of other men, attended by love. I, in this room, separate, alienated, distrustful, find in my purpose not an open world, but a closed, hopeless jail' (8 January).

This alienation is expressed in a series of conflicts with the world outside him as he explores his revulsion from the material world, the social world, and from sexual and emotional engagement. The ugliness of the Chicago slums has its analogue in the capacity for cruel meanness that he discovers at the Servatius party in those friends whom he had thought of as forming a 'colony of the spirit' that would protect him from the crudity and danger of the world. He finds a similar meanness in his niece Etta, and sees only condescension in his brother Amos's attempts at generosity. He drifts away from his mistress Kitty Daumler when he finds that he has become important to her, and he shows little affection for and no erotic interest in his wife Iva who is, in fact, remarkably long-suffering. His hopeless state is reflected in those around him: in the 'queer, annoying creature' Vanaker, as enclosed and aimless as Joseph; in the exiled, shabby woman who sells Christian Science literature; in his landlady, who is simply waiting to die. Joseph's withdrawals from the external world are re-enacted internally when he stands apart from his own past, from 'that older self' who had inhabited the external world and who believed in a 'common humanity'. That older Joseph saw himself as a visionary, and had developed a plan for his life, a shape for his future that had involved the shaping also of his friends and his family and that had meant the denial of pessimism.

Joseph's attempt to withdraw from his past self can be seen as an attempted separation from history and an assertion of his own special status, and on one level it is possible to sympathize with his denial of complicity in the absurdity that he now sees around him. But the novel makes it clear that Joseph's vision of the world and himself is suspect. His disappointment with his friends, his sense that he has somehow been betrayed by them, must be seen in the light of his own irrational bursts of anger. Why does Jimmy Burns ignore him? Presumably it has something to do with Joseph's departure from the revolutionary party to which they had once both belonged, but Joseph takes it personally, as a tacit denial of his identity, and makes a scene. Brooding on the event afterwards, he is upset by the response of his friend Myron Adler who witnessed the scene:

It seemed to me that Myron might have been somewhat less worried about the spectacle I had made of myself and the attention I had drawn to him and more concerned about the cause of my outburst. . . . But then, I may be expecting too much from Myron. He has the pride of what he has become: a successful young man, comfortable, respected, safe for the present from those craters of the spirit which I have lately looked into.   (22 December)

Thus Myron is aligned with Burns as one who has denied him. The same thing happens when his wife is upset by the spectacle he makes of himself at his brother's house: ' "Dearest," I shouted. "It's so nice to know that you at least have faith in me!" ' (26 December). Joseph's sense of his own importance is accompanied by a belief that others fail to recognize it. His response to Burns is essentially paranoid. At many points in the novel it is indicated that Joseph feels that his identity is being denied: by Frink the bank manager, by his niece Etta, by the waitress who refuses to take back his burned toast, by Marie, the maid, who smokes in his presence because, Joseph thinks, she recognizes that he is of no importance, and by those friends who, he believes, have failed him by revealing their own susceptibility to pettiness, to rage and spite.

Although Joseph may deny his own complicity in these aspects of 'common humanity', he cannot completely conceal it. Almost immediately after his account of the Servatius party that caused him so much disappointment comes his confrontation with Etta. His niece has no respect for him because of his poverty, and she is, he is right in thinking, a thoroughly mean girl, but this does not justify his beating of her. He remains, however, oblivious to the irony given to his action by his meditation on the Haydn divertimento that he was listening to when she interrupted him:

Its sober opening notes, preliminaries to a thoughtful confession, showed me that I was still an apprentice in suffering and humiliation. I had not even begun. I had, furthermore, no right to expect to avoid them. So much was immediately clear. Surely no one could plead for exception; that was not a human privilege. What I should do with them, how to meet them, was answered in the second declaration: with grace, without meanness.   (26 December)

Joseph fails to act 'with grace, without meanness'; worse, he fails to recognize or understand his failure.

Joseph's conflict with the world is finally internalized in the form of a debate that he conducts with an alter-ego that he creates for himself, a Spirit of Alternatives. Through this confrontation with himself Joseph scrutinizes the whole question of his alienation, approaching a recognition that he does live in the world and that he must learn to see it as it is, without ideal constructions, without the false protection of a colony of the spirit; and, more crucially, that he has no separate destiny, that his stance of isolation and 'freedom' is a posture. But this is something he is not ready for, and he withdraws once again from an acknowledgement of this truth.

So how *is* a good man to live? For all his agonized self-scrutiny there is much in himself that Joseph fails to see, and it is clear that the old Joseph, from whom he has mockingly detached himself, was a better man than the new one. His final decision to ask the draft board to call him up immediately is, as he recognizes himself, a surrender, a sign of his failure. He has had freedom, and has used it for a morbid and paralysing search for its own meaning. By allowing himself to be absorbed into the great masses of the army, to become another of those who do as they are told, he acknowledges his inability to answer his own question. This ending has caused a certain amount of critical disagreement. Keith Opdahl sees it as a failure because it does not reconcile Joseph's acceptance of an evil world with his need for 'an essential, transcendent self', creating a conflict in Bellow's own art; Robert Dutton, however, thinks that it shows a recognition of social necessity, that we are a part of the world and cannot separate ourselves from it.[21] But there is, surely, in the novel's final words, an intentional ambiguity, a deep irony in Joseph's announcement of his capitulation, that arises from his awareness of his own inadequacy:

> Hurray for regular hours!
> And for the supervision of the spirit!
> Long live regimentation!

He knows what he is doing, and his act, capitulation though it may be, is also a rejection of alienation and a return to the firmer ground of the world, where a new start to his struggle may be made. He is, like the dangling button that so concerns him, ready to be sewn back into place.

The problematic ambiguity of the novel's ending arises in part from the narrative form that Bellow employed. The device of a journal allows for only a single point of view, which encloses the reader's perspective within Joseph's, and encourages him to assume that the author's own point of view is identical with that of the narrator. This creates difficulties in gauging the extent to which the fictional world actually is as Joseph sees it; there is, as we have noted, much evidence that his perceptions are distorted, in the various inconsistencies in his judgements, and in the parallels and mirror-images placed in the narrative, but there is no way for us to decide how far this distortion extends, and consequently the novel's conclusion leaves us with a paradox that cannot be resolved. In his second novel Bellow partially solved this problem by offering a more complex perspective: we see things from the point of view of its protagonist, Asa Leventhal, but the narrative voice is located at an ironic distance outside him, so that we have some means of assessing the reliability of his perspective.

Insofar as *Dangling Man* is a 'Jewish' novel, its concerns are with the experience of the Jewish intellectual living in an urban environment from which he feels estranged. Asa Leventhal, the protagonist of *The Victim*, has similar feelings of alienation, though he is by no means an intellectual. However, it would hardly have been possible for Bellow to write about Jewish experience in what is essentially a war-time novel – he had produced two drafts of *The Victim* by 1945, and its final version was published in 1947 – without confronting the enormity of the Holocaust. The novel reflects upon the roots of anti-Semitism, and although it does not treat the Holocaust directly, it is haunted by those six million deaths and the irrational hatred that caused them. It does not deal with anti-Semitism in a recriminatory way, however; rather, it looks at the conditions under which men see others as their enemies; and it considers the responsibility for himself and for others that a man must shoulder if he is to live in society. This is indicated in the novel's two epigraphs. The first, a passage from the *Thousand and One Nights*, concerns a merchant who, by violently throwing away date-stones, unwittingly kills the son of an Ifrit, an act for which the Ifrit demands the merchant's life in compensation. The implication of this epigraph is that a man is responsible for all harm that he does to others, even harm of which he is unconscious. The second is an extract from Thomas De Quincey's *The Pains of Opium*, which reveals a paranoid vision of the agonized masses of mankind pressing upwards as if to overwhelm the viewer. What is implied by this epigraph is more complex, for although it clearly relates to Asa Leventhal's fears about threats to his own individual identity, it is, in its original context, part of a drug-induced hallucination, and consequently raises questions about the reality of subjective perception.

The main plot of *The Victim* presents its protagonist's bewildered struggle with a hitherto unperceived enemy, Kirby Allbee. Leventhal is a middle-class Jewish newspaper editor, left alone in New York because his wife has gone to look after her mother. His solitude encourages morbid self-pity and emotional disorientation, making him particularly vulnerable to the charges of his old acquaintance Allbee, whom he meets one day in a park. Allbee accuses Leventhal of being the cause of the loss of his job, and of his resulting physical and social disintegration. Some years earlier, at a time when Leventhal was unemployed, Allbee had arranged an interview for him with his employer Rudiger; Leventhal, annoyed by Rudiger's contemptuous treatment of him, had created a scene and this, according to Allbee, had caused Rudiger to fire him. Allbee believes that Leventhal is a member of a Jewish network that is gathering all privilege to itself, and that Leventhal caused his dismissal intentionally. Although Allbee's accusations seem absurd, Leventhal nevertheless feels obscurely guilty, and as he delves into the story he becomes increasingly aware that he might be to blame, and therefore increasingly unable to resist Allbee's recriminations and demands, eventually allowing him to move into his apartment. When one day Leventhal discovers Allbee in the apartment with a woman, he throws him out; Allbee returns and attempts to gas both himself and Leventhal, but is once again driven away, this time permanently. The two meet once again, some years later; Leventhal is much happier and more secure, and Allbee, though socially better placed, is no less degenerate. In the interlocking sub-plot, Leventhal resentfully takes responsibility for his sister-in-law Elena and her sick son Mickey because his brother Max is working away from home. He convinces himself that the Catholic Elena and her mother resent him because he is a Jew, and that they blame him when the boy dies. At the same time, however, he develops a protective and redeeming interest in his other nephew Philip.

The novel is built upon the conflict between the Jewish protagonist and his anti-Semitic persecutor, but as it progresses it blurs the distinctions between the two, making Allbee into a kind of alter-ego or double for Leventhal, and creating a puzzle out of the question of who is the 'victim' of the title. This relationship is carefully, even schematically developed, as the paranoid vision of the anti-Semitic Allbee (whose obsession with Jews has given him a greater understanding of Jewish culture than Leventhal appears to have) duplicates Leventhal's own paranoia. The larger implications of this relationship mean that it is developed on a symbolic rather than a realistic level. The two men are brought together in a series of scenes that link them in carefully worked out stages. On first meeting Allbee in the park Leventhal finds that he remembers his name easily, even though he has not seen him for some years or thought much about him and even though he generally has a poor memory for names. Later, during a visit to the zoo with his nephew Philip, there is a moment when Leventhal identifies with Allbee:

> [Leventhal] was so conscious of Allbee, so certain he was being scrutinized, that he was able to see himself as if through a strange pair of eyes: the side of his face, the palpitation in his throat, the seams of his skin, the shape of his body and of his feet in their white shoes. Changed in this way into his own observer, he was able to see Allbee, too. (Ch. 9)

He seems to be at one and the same time Allbee watching himself and himself watching Allbee. This feeling of sharing his identity is repeated just before Leventhal accepts Allbee into his house as a 'guest', when he suddenly feels the 'intimate nearness' of Allbee, 'and the look of recognition Allbee bent on him duplicated the look in his own' (Ch. 13).

Leventhal's growing awareness of Allbee becomes a sort of love. In spite of the revulsion the two feel for each other there is, just before the novel's climax, a mutual recognition of something beyond their differences:

> Allbee bent forward and laid his hand on the arm of Leventhal's chair, and for a short space the two men looked at each other and Leventhal felt himself singularly drawn with a kind of affection. It oppressed him, it was repellent. . . . However it did not seem just then a serious fault. (Ch. 19)

This recognition gives meaning to the climactic moment when Allbee tries to gas himself and Leventhal. ' "You want to murder

me? Murder?"' a horrified Leventhal asks, to which Allbee, 'as if
with his last breath,' replies: ' "Me, myelf!" ' (Ch. 23). It is deliber-
ately left unclear whether Allbee wants to kill himself, or to destroy
what he sees of himself in Leventhal – although in the book's final
chapter the narrator, in a rare intrusion of opinion, says of this
'suicide pact' that Allbee did not intend to die himself – but this
moment of symbolic death frees Leventhal from his alter ego, and
allows him a rebirth into a new awareness, however limited, of his
participation in the suffering of others.

Some readers of *The Victim* have found this symbolic mode hard
to take. Alan S. Downer, in reviewing the novel when it first
appeared, attacked it for the contrivance of its structure, a contrivance which, he felt, confused rather than clarified its meaning.[22]
Reuben Frank, with a little more generosity, thought that the novel
came off 'more as an intellectual statement than as the problems of
living human beings'.[23] The structure itself derives from earlier
'double' literature, from such works as Conrad's short story 'The
Secret Sharer', from Dostoevsky's story 'The Double' and, more
immediately, from Dostoevsky's novel *The Eternal Husband*, from
which Bellow adapted the main plot of *The Victim*. The double in
Bellow's novel is not, however, a straight projection of the protagonist's darker motives, a kind of 'evil twin'; Allbee is not simply an
embodiment of evil. It is easier to see how Bellow intends Allbee to
be understood if we note that he also has roots in the Spirit of
Alternatives that Joseph created for himself in *Dangling Man*, to
whom he gave the name 'Tu As Raison Aussi' – 'You're Right Too'.

This is not to deny that Allbee is a villain. He has a distorted
vision of the world, he judges and acts according to that vision, and
his actions are destructive because of the nature of the distortion.
But the distortion is clearly explained in the novel. Allbee makes a
claim to 'nobility': he comes from a patrician family, claiming
Governor Winthrop as one of his ancestors, and has been brought
up to assume the right to the privileges of power; further, he has
talents or virtues that, at least in the past, have made a good
impression, so that his friends the Willistons are unwilling to
believe Leventhal's stories about him. But he has a weak character
and, mixing alcoholism with arrogance, has destroyed his career
and his marriage. Indubitably, he has suffered, and he is bewildered because he cannot understand the reasons for his suffering.
He therefore magnifies the importance of Leventhal's confrontation with Rudiger and locates the cause of his own subsequent

failure in Leventhal, whose apparent success he believes to be protected by a Jewish network. That is, he conflates a faulty reading of immediate social reality with an ancient and irrational idea of the Jew, the child of Caliban, as the enemy of Western civilization, 'alien in his habits, his pursuits, his interests, his character, his very blood'.[24]

But Leventhal too sees himself as persecuted by forces outside himself; he also judges by the light of a faulty view of the world. It is this complication of the issues of right and wrong in the central relationship of the novel that gives it meaning. Leventhal is not presented as a particularly attractive or admirable character. He is large and heavy, physically at odds with a world in which he is constantly knocking against objects. His physical heaviness reflects an intellectual and spiritual clumsiness: he possesses an intelligence 'not greatly interested in its own powers, as if preferring not to be bothered by them, indifferent; and this indifference appeared to be extended to others' (Ch. 2). The indifference, however, is a front for a turmoil of fears. Leventhal feels the guilt that the anti-Semite imposes upon the Jew, feels that in some way he deserves to be persecuted. These feelings colour his perception of the world around him, so that the persecution seems real. He has fears about his position in society that amount to paranoia: he has once seen 'the bottom', while working as a clerk in a flophouse, and thinks that perhaps that is where he belongs. He fears that he occupies a position in his middle-class world that does not belong to him, and that he, as a Jew, has been and continues to be persecuted by forces working through a black-list that was used against him when he was looking for a job; he attempts to verify the existence of this on a number of occasions. We are told of all these fears before Allbee makes his appearance. In addition, at the moment at which the novel opens Leventhal is shown to be in an unusually vulnerable condition. The absence of his wife, whom we do not meet until the end of the book but who clearly is the principle of order in his life, has left him with the feeling that he is lost in an alien and hostile universe.

Neither Allbee nor Leventhal sees things as they are, and the stylistic fabric of *The Victim* underscores their perverse social vision. In *Dangling Man* the monochrome dullness of the Chicago winter landscape reflected the 'narcotic dullness' of Joseph's own state. Here, the infernal strangeness of the New York summer is presented from the outset, through images of fire and darkness, of heat and wildness, as a correlative of Leventhal's state of mind:

> On some nights New York is as hot as Bangkok. The whole
> continent seems to have moved from its place and slid nearer the
> equator, the bitter grey Atlantic to have become green and
> tropical, and the people, thronging the streets, barbaric fellahin
> among the stupendous monuments of their mystery, the lights of
> which, a dazing profusion, climb upward endlessly into the heat
> of the sky.

This, the novel's opening paragraph, contains images of slippage,
of dislocation and inversion, as well as the implied threat of the
'barbaric fellahin', that provide a key to the distortion of the way in
which Leventhal and Allbee see things.

Most of the main issues of the novel centre on this idea of
distorted vision, and they relate closely to a recurrent theatrical
metaphor. A spectator at a theatre watches something that is not
'reality', though it may pretend to be reality, and it may have a
meaning in relation to reality. The spectator has to avoid being
taken in by its illusion, however; to understand what he sees he has
to be able to judge it correctly. At the centre of this metaphor are
two discussions that occur in scenes that may seem to be digressions, the first in a restaurant amongst a group of men who are
vaguely connected with the theatre, the second at a birthday party
held for the niece of Leventhal's friend Harkavy; both of them
feature an elderly writer called Schlossberg. In the first of these
scenes, at the restaurant, Schlossberg develops an argument about
the nature of good acting, asserting that 'Good acting is what is
exactly human' (Ch. 10). This is a rather enigmatic statement, since
it seems to contradict itself, equating the truly human with the truly
artificial, but Schlossberg goes on to show that good acting represents the authentic and appropriate response to human experience, which he defines as 'dignity'. In the scene at the party, during
a discussion about funerals, Schlossberg tells of the last funeral he
attended, at which paper grass had been put down to hide the dirt
of the grave. This, says Schlossberg, is an attempt to evade the
reality of death, to be more than human. He concludes with
another apparent enigma: 'paper grass in the grave makes all the
grass paper' (Ch. 21). Presumably he means by this that delusion
begins with self-delusion, and that an attempt to deny one reality
brings all other reality into question.

The question arises from this of how much Leventhal learns. He certainly recognizes that Allbee is not 'exactly human', referring to him more than once as a bad actor. And his discovery that he has been mistaken in believing Elena and her mother to be hostile to him (indeed, that his error arose in part from his own hostility to their Catholicism) makes him at least question whether other of his perceptions have been wrong, and tempers his attitude towards Allbee. Some critics have found the novel's conclusion to be optimistic, with Leventhal 'joining humanity without surrendering to society'.[25] Others see Leventhal as being more comfortable with himself, but neither much changed nor any wiser.[26] The final chapter, appropriately set in a theatre, certainly seems to indicate that, while he feels more at peace with himself, he does not really see things much more clearly than he did before his experience with Allbee. The final passage has him ask Allbee 'what's your idea of who runs things?' The question remains unanswered, and as the theatre lights go down Leventhal is left literally and figuratively in the dark.

Leventhal's question, however, indicates what it is that is at the root of his problem. He and Allbee have both held contradictory views about how things are run, each believing both that there is an arbitrary fate and that there is a hostile conspiracy of powerful interests. These irrational anxieties arise out of the fragility of their sense of self (they lack Schlossberg's 'dignity'), and particularly of their sense of social identity. Leventhal is well aware of his closeness to 'the lost, the outcast, the overcome, the effaced, the ruined,' and believes he is not amongst them only because he has 'got away with it' (Ch. 2). Allbee, in this view, has not got away with it. But both are, in fact, the victims of social reality, and Bellow knows this, even if they do not. Leventhal's question about who runs things suggests possibly metaphysical or transcendent answers: God? Fate? But the novel provides a more material answer. In the world of *The Victim* hierarchical patterns are not properly perceived, for while it may be a misinterpretation for 'the victim' (Leventhal or Allbee) to see a conspiracy behind his suffering, the fact is that, like any who are powerless, Jewish *or* anti-Semitic, he *is* a victim of certain social realities. These are that power protects and consolidates itself (Beard is not above nepotism), and that those who have power may well abuse those who do not (Leventhal's response to Rudiger may have been unacceptable, but it was provoked by totally unjustifiable behaviour on Rudiger's part). To begin to understand 'who runs things', therefore, to make a move towards the dignity of being 'exactly human', it is necessary for a man first of all to recognize that there may be distortions in his own vision: he has to rid himself of his paper grass. He may then be able to take control of his own destiny.

Dangling Man and *The Victim* are remarkable for the intensity of their introversion, for the way in which the perceived world reflects the mental state of the mind that perceives it, and perhaps they imply that there is no possibility of a world independent of the eye/I that sees it. However, this insistent focus on the experience of the protagonist does exclude certain possibilities. One of these, as we have seen, is the possibility of a wide and complex perspective. Another problem is that, despite the comic potential of their fictional material, the two books constantly shy away from comedy. Indeed, at one point *The Victim* actually articulates this avoidance: after Leventhal has ejected Allbee and the woman from his home his immediate response is relieved laughter at what is, after all, a ludicrous scene; immediately, however, he denies his own response: 'when he sat down for a moment on the bed, all the comedy of it was snatched away and torn to pieces' (Ch. 23). It is as if Bellow were inhibited by Leventhal, as if the solemnity of the protagonist had somehow taken over the vision of the book, refusing the comic possibilities. Whether or not these missed possibilities are seen as faults, however, these two early novels are still worth serious attention.

3

Novels of the Fifties

The fundamental source of the gloom of Bellow's forties novels must be located in his response to the times, to the years of the Depression and the war, and the essentially European models that he used were appropriate for the experience of those two books. His next novel marked a radical change of direction: *The Adventures of Augie March* (1953) is a vast comic sprawl of a work, crammed with characters and ideas, its material constantly threatening to burst out of its form. The change in attitude may be accounted for at least in part by the historical moment of its writing, a time of high expectations associated with post-war reconstruction and the liberal optimism of the early years of the Eisenhower administration. Bellow's travels in Europe in the late forties, during which some of the novel was composed, must also have had a liberating effect on him, contributing to his interest in the European roots of America's immigrants, something which is hardly reflected at all in the earlier novels. Bellow remains concerned with issues of identity, freedom and responsibility. In *Dangling Man*, however, Joseph pursued the question of his 'separate destiny' by eschewing the external world and looking inwards, within the claustrophobic enclosure of his room; and Leventhal's discoveries about his connectedness to the larger society were also the product of a painful introversion. Augie, in contrast, tries to locate his identity by constant experience of the external, social world, and this accounts for the open, inclusive form of the novel. Some measure of the distance Bellow has come can be gauged by the way in which he treats the issue that haunted *The Victim*, creating the dark threat fundamental to its tone: although *The Adventures of Augie March* is a Jewish novel, the question of anti-Semitism hardly arises in it. It is raised and dismissed in the opening chapter, when Augie tells of how he and his brothers were occasionally stoned or beaten up for being 'Christ-killers' but goes on to comment: 'I never had any special grief from it, or brooded, being by and large too larky and boisterous to take it to heart'.

This is not the novel that Bellow originally intended should follow *The Victim*; he started on a 'grim' work to be entitled *The Crab and the Butterfly*, of which he wrote a substantial part, but he became depressed by it, and finally scrapped it.[27] Part of this work was published as a story called 'The Trip to Galena' (1950). Its protagonist, Weyl, is clearly related to Joseph of *Dangling Man*, an aimless, suffering intellectual alienated from the world; he struggles to find meaning within himself, without much success. This is one of a number of short stories Bellow produced while he was working on *Augie March*; two others, 'A Sermon by Doctor Pep' (1949) and 'An Address by Gooley MacDowell to the Hasbeens Club of Chicago' (1951) are virtuoso monologues spoken by eccentric self-proclaimed experts on life of the kind who fill *Augie March*, and indeed a number of sections of the novel first appeared as short stories, including those concerning Einhorn, Mintouchian, and Basteshaw.

Clearly, Bellow was experimenting with different voices, and building towards that most dynamic voice of Augie March himself. At the same time he was in need of a less constricting form than those he had previously used, which he now rejected as the product of an immature and self-conscious art unsuited to his talents: 'Why should I force myself to write like an Englishman or a contributor to the New Yorker? I soon saw that it was simply not in me to be a mandarin'.[28] A more accommodating, if riskier, form seemed necessary to trap the texture of contemporary life: 'I kicked over the traces, wrote catch-as-catch can, picaresque. I took my chance'.[29] Bellow's new venture met with immediate acclaim. In his review of *Augie March* Robert Penn Warren called it 'by far the best' of Bellow's books and suggested that 'from now on any discussion of fiction in America in our time will have to take account of it'. Norman Podhoretz, while pointing to the novel's weaknesses, nevertheless concluded that it had 'the very genuine distinction of giving us a sense of what a real American idiom might look like'.[30] The novel received the National Book Award for that year.

The Adventures of Augie March takes its protagonist from the Chicago of the Depression, through Mexico, to post-war Europe, and from a boyhood 'larkiness' to a more mature (though perhaps unsuccessful) search for meaning in the world. His experiences cover many activities and occupations that take him into most levels of society. His jobs include working as Santa's elf in a department store, as factotum for the crippled 'genius' Einhorn, as doggroomer, as coal merchant, as salesman of riding equipment and of rubberized paint. He steals and sells books, helps to manage a prize-fighter, becomes a tramp for a brief time, works as a union organizer, trains an eagle to hunt iguanas, almost becomes involved with Trotsky, joins the Merchant Marine and is set adrift in a lifeboat. He picks up an education through occasional courses, through life-experience and through a voracious appetite for reading. He lives in expatriate communities in Mexico and Europe. He has affairs with a number of women, almost marrying one for her money, and falling in love with two more. And he meets a great profusion of colourful people.

It must be clear that this vast and various mass of material resists easy formal containment. Bellow himself referred to the form of his book as 'picaresque'. The conventional picaresque novel is structured on the experiences of its central character, the *picaro*, and is therefore often presented in the form of an autobiography. The *picaro* is a rogue, usually of low birth, who lives by his wits. He functions in a world that is realistically depicted, and gets involved in a series of adventures that have no necessary connection, but are used to mock the social types with whom he comes into contact. All this is generally true of *Augie March*, but one aspect of the traditional *picaro* raises questions: he does not usually undergo any character development. There are indeed readings of this book that argue that Augie does not develop, but most critics have noted change in his character; Keith Opdahl, asserting that Augie 'turns inward and discovers himself – and gains substance as a character', claims that the book is really a *Bildungsroman*.[31] This is a form of novel that details the progress of a young man to maturity, and like the picaresque it is usually autobiographical; however, here the protagonist does undergo a development of character, and the novel derives its structure from this learning process. In spite of their similarities it would appear that these two forms are mutually exclusive, since one places emphasis on the external world, the other on the inner development of its protagonist. Nevertheless, there is a sense in which *The Adventures of Augie March* is trying to be both things, and part of its effect as well as some of its problems arise from a tension between the two.

This problematic relationship between the novel's inner and outer worlds raises questions about how the narrative voice is to be understood. Augie March is the narrator of his own story, and since the voice he speaks with often sounds as if it might be Bellow's own it is difficult to judge the extent to which he has authorial approval. A further complication is that he is telling his story in retrospect, and this, although it gives ironic distance, tends to confuse the issue of whether the developments that take place in Augie's character during the course of his adventures are caused by his immediate experiences, or whether they are superimposed by the acquired wisdom of the older narrator. Bellow had faced similar problems with the narrative point of view in his earlier novels; here he tries to open up the perspective by making Augie the object of judgement by such acute intelligences as Einhorn, Thea and Tambow. Nevertheless there are still, as we shall see, problems about how Augie can finally be understood.

Like Joseph, Augie wishes to believe that he has a separate destiny, or special fate. 'A man's character is his fate', Augie tells us in the novel's opening paragraph, and he therefore has to believe in his own particular distinction (this is implied in his name: 'August' = 'exalted'). At the same time, Bellow seems to conceive of Augie as in some ways typical, representing a general modern American experience: 'I am an American, Chicago born – Chicago, that somber city – and go at things as I have taught myself, free style, and will make the record in my own way' (5). Augie's robust opening statement contains the traditional American stance of democratic independence but embodies it in the figure of the urban immigrant. Chicago, that teeming, violent city (it is curious that Augie calls Chicago 'somber'; the adjective applies very well to the Chicago of *Dangling Man*, but Augie's Chicago is fertile and vital), represents the great material mass of urban America.

Both the character of Augie and the world in which he operates are represented to us through the novel's highly distinctive style, which is inseparable from the narrative voice. The significance of this can best be understood by looking at the source of much that is in this book, the poetry of Walt Whitman. At one point in the novel Augie characterizes himself as being 'democratic in temperament, available to everybody and assuming about others what I assumed about myself' (Ch. 8). This is a direct reference to the opening lines of Whitman's 'Song of Myself':

I celebrate myself, and sing myself,
And what I assume you shall assume,

For every atom belonging to me as good belongs to you.

In this poem Whitman is presenting himself not just as an American, but as the sum total of American experience:

> Of every hue and caste am I, of every rank and religion,
> A farmer, mechanic, artist, gentleman, sailors, quaker,
> Prisoner, fancy-man, rowdy, lawyer, physician, priest.
>
> (Section 16)

One of the effects of Augie's having so many occupations, of his experiencing American life on so many social levels, is to give him the same kind of representative status as the voice of Whitman's poem gives to itself: both are presented as the embodiment of American diversity. There is a nice irony in this, however, for what gave Whitman the conviction of his own representativeness was his sense of security, of being rooted in American history, as we see if we turn again to the opening of his poem:

> My tongue, every atom of my blood, form'd from this soil,
> this air,
> Born here of parents born here from parents the same, and
> their parents the same.

Bellow has adapted the Whitmanesque voice and stance for a different kind of American, one with no roots in the country's history (Augie's lack of such rooted security is signified not only by his being of an immigrant family, but also by the absence of a father); he is, in effect, redefining America.

Bellow's use of Whitman goes beyond this, however, for the stylistic device he employs most frequently in his construction of the external world of the novel – the catalogue, or list – is also borrowed from the poet. It is as if Bellow believed that the only way in which the immense variety and confusion of the material surface of the world could be recorded were by a constant amassing of detail, often apparently random. The lists may represent human variety, like the 'clumpers, cripples, hunchbacks, brace-legs, crutch-wielders, tooth and eye sufferers, and all the rest' (Ch. 1) who attend the dispensary; or the slum-born children of immigrants, 'Bohunk wizards at the Greeks, demon-brained physicists, historians bred under pushcarts, and many hard-grain poor boys

who were going to starve and work themselves bitterly eight years
or so to become doctors, engineers, scholars, and experts' (Ch. 8)
who attend the city college. Similar lists may generate the peculiar
atmosphere of a place, like the feeling of shady, energetic greed for
wealth and power associated with Chicago's City Hall, with its
'bigshots and operators, commissioners, grabbers, heelers, tipsters,
hoodlums, wolves, fixers, plaintiffs, flatfeet, men in Western hats
and women in lizard shoes and fur coats' (Ch. 3). Augie's catalogue
of the odds and ends on Einhorn's desk indicates the nature of
Einhorn's business interests, but it also helps to define his character: 'wire trays labeled Incoming and Outgoing, molten Aetna
weights, notary's seal on a chain, staplers, flap-moistening sponges,
keys to money, confidential papers, notes, condoms, personal
correspondence and poems and essays' (Ch. 5). The jumble of
ordinary office equipment, the mixing of business papers with
poems, the sly intrusion of that word 'condoms' to indicate the
priapic compulsions of this cripple – this is more than just a list.
The same is true of the description of Simon's apartment: 'there
were vast rugs and table lamps as tall as life-sized dolls or female
idols, walls that were all mahogany, drawers full of underwear and
shirts, sliding doors that opened on racks of shoes, on rows of coats,
cases of gloves, of socks, bottles of eau de cologne, little caskets,
lights lining the corners' (Ch. 21). The attraction of wealth is
apparent here, but the profusion also implies its own emptiness
and explains Simon's self-destructive frustration with what wealth
has brought to him.

   At one point, while in the middle of a set of lists defining the
Coblin household, Augie tells us that the Coblins are 'hipped on
superabundance' (26), and his statement might be appropriate as
an explanation of Bellow's technique. This technique can be called
'realistic', since it aims at representing actuality. It has a moral
dimension also, for it implies an equation of realism with materialism that has much to do with the worldly attitudes that Augie tries
to counter. Bellow had originally intended to call his novel *Life
Among the Machiavellians*, because it sets Augie in motion in a world
of 'realists', of characters who think they see and understand the
world as it is and wish to control it through manipulation and
deception. These Machiavellians try to direct Augie's gaze to what
they think of as reality and by doing so to form him as they wish
him to be. Grandma Lausch, the first of these, has a vision of a
world of 'the trustful, loving, and simple surrounded by the

cunning-hearted and tough ... a desperate mankind without feelings' (Ch. 1). Augie's career is a succession of confrontations with such realists: Einhorn, Simon, Mrs Renling, Thea, Mintouchian, Basteshaw are amongst the largest of many who try to wear him down and 'determine' him until he has to say (characteristically in another catalogue), 'To tell the truth, I'm good and tired of all these big personalities, heavy-water brains, Machiavellis and wizard evil-doers, big-wheels and imposers upon, absolutists' (Ch. 26). Augie himself is an idealist, motivated by love, with a conception of himself as having a higher, individual fate; he wishes to be like Trotsky, to navigate by 'the great stars', to be 'fit to speak the most important human words and universal terms' (Ch. 17).

In spite of his individualism Augie is a curiously passive, insubstantial character. Robert Penn Warren attributed this shadowiness to the fact that 'it is hard to give substance to a character who has no commitments, and by definition Augie is the man with no commitments'.[32] Augie hardly ever initiates anything; rather, things are done to him as others make their impositions upon him: a recurring image in the book is of Augie being dressed by someone, by Mrs Renling, by Thea, even by his brother Simon. In each case he wears the clothing, the imposed identity, for a time, but always finally withdraws. The result of this pattern of entry and withdrawal is that the novel has a rhythm rather than a structure. But there is another cause of the problems in Augie's characterization which we can see if we go back to the questions raised earlier in connection with Bellow's attempts to adapt elements of the picaresque and the *Bildungsroman* to his own ends. The protagonist of a picaresque novel is essentially a device, used to present and satirize the external social world, while the protagonist of a *Bildungsroman* is a fully realized character with a real inner life who must live in relation to his own beliefs. In *The Adventures of Augie March* the conflicting requirements of the two forms have set up a corresponding conflict in the central figure who is a character who must sometimes function as a device.

As a device, Augie is employed to examine the ways in which others survive and triumph in the predatory material world. He and his brothers represent various possible ways of living. Simon March embraces fully the methods of the Machiavellians and their material values, and in so doing becomes a slave to money; his increasing physical and moral grossness makes him almost an emblem of the novel's materialism, yet like Fitzgerald's Jay Gatsby

he generates sympathy in the reader, who can see him as a victim of
the 'American dream'. Georgy March represents a passive simplicity that makes nothing of the material world, and is related to the
victimized self-sacrificing love of the Marches' mother. Late in the
novel Augie envies the simplicity of Georgy's life, but it is a
simplicity that is unavailable to Augie because it derives from
unconsciousness of reality and the inadequacy of the idiot. Augie is
as drawn by the seductive attractions of wealth as Simon is, but
those seductions are not powerful enough to overcome his belief
that he has a higher personal destiny, a belief which generates in
him what Einhorn calls 'opposition', a refusal to go along with the
current of the world. This quality is well illustrated when, for
purely altruistic reasons, he involves himself in Mimi Villars's
attempts to procure an abortion, knowing that he will destroy his
chance to marry into the wealthy Magnus family. It is at moments
like this that he functions as a character rather than a device. The
problem is that there is insufficient energy in this opposition to give
Augie the kind of substance he needs, for the fact is that most of
the time he is *not* in opposition. He goes along with Simon's plan
for him to marry Lucy Magnus even though he is well aware of the
improbability of his finding happiness in such a union, and is only
saved from it by what is essentially an accident, Mimi's need for an
abortion. He lives as a dress-up doll for Mrs Renling and only
releases himself from her when she wants to adopt him, offering
no better explanation than that 'it wasn't a fate good enough for
me' (Ch. 9). He believes that he loves Thea, and allows her too to
dress him up, but he is not the predator that she wants him to be,
and his escape from her is precipitated by another accident.

This division in the concept of Augie's character may also
account for the problems with the ending. As with the two earlier
novels, the conclusion of this one has aroused a degree of critical
hostility, since it does not seem to be justified by what has led up to
it. Leslie Fiedler, for example, says of the apparently unearned
affirmation of the ending: '*Augie*, which begins with such rightness,
such conviction, does not know how to end; shriller and shriller,
wilder and wilder, it finally whirls apart in a frenzy of fake
euphoria and exclamatory prose'.[33] In the picaresque novel, there
is no character development, which means that the protagonist
ends as he began, and the requirements of this novel's rhythmic
form necessitate an optimistic ending. Augie's experience hardly
gives him cause for optimism; if there is any lesson to be learned

from his experiences, it is that there is no happiness to be found in life, or, as Kayo Obermark tells him, 'Everyone has bitterness in his chosen thing' (Ch. 12). Yet Augie persists in clinging to the view of human possibility that he had articulated in response to Mimi's claims that for most people there is only suffering:

> Me, I couldn't think all was so poured in concrete and that there weren't occasions for happiness that weren't illusions of people still permitted to be forgetful of permanent disappointment, more or less permanent pain, death of children, lovers, friends, ends of causes, old age, loathsome breath, fallen faces, white hair, retreated breasts, dropped teeth; and maybe most intolerable the hardening of detestable character, like bone, similar to a second skeleton and creaking loudest before the end. (Ch. 12)

The interesting point here is that despite its affirmation what remains memorable about this passage is what it says about the pain of the human condition.

The same is true of the novel's conclusion. Augie, who for so long resisted the siren call of materialism, is working for the cynic Mintouchian at the shadier end of the business world. The man who had wanted to navigate by the great stars is hitched to Stella, the shallow 'star'; the idealist who had thought of opening a school and of shaping the future through children is, and appears likely to remain, childless, with no stake in the future. He ends his story by presenting himself as a Columbus, the rediscoverer of America: 'I may well be a flop at this line of endeavor. Columbus too thought he was a flop, probably, when they sent him back in chains. Which didn't prove there was no America'. But if Augie is a Columbus, he is a Columbus in exile, saluting America from the bitter chill of Europe. Augie is defeated, and the 'fake euphoria' if that is what this is, is Augie's, not Bellow's, and it arises out of the tension generated by the competing pressures of, on the one hand, the literary device that represents unchanging idealism, and on the other the 'living' character that responds to experience and is modified by it.

We cannot leave *Augie March* without saying something about the women in it. In the two earlier novels the female characters are generally sketchily developed; even the protagonists' wives, though they are sympathetic creations, are relegated to the margins of the story. In *Augie March*, however, we are presented with many vivid female characters. Bellow has frequently been criticized for the female figures he creates, who (especially in the later novels) are often wish-fulfilment beauties seen from a misogynist perspective, like Madeleine Herzog, Denise Citrine or Matilda Layamon, erotic and destructive. All, however, are seen from the point of view of a narrator who has been bruised by them. The women with whom Augie gets involved are in some respects unconvincing; most are stunningly beautiful and fall easily in love with Augie. Sophie, self-sacrificing to an improbable degree, is unappreciated by Augie; Thea, whom he loves, wishes to re-create him in her own predatory image; and Stella, whom he finally marries, turns out (to Augie as well as the reader) to be pathetically dishonest and superficial. However, Bellow seems to be playing a game with the allegorical suggestions of the names of these women: Sophie ('wisdom') is rejected by Augie, while Thea ('goddess') and Stella ('star') – we might add also Lucy ('light'), whom he almost marries for her money – all imply something ideal, but also illusory. Seen from this perspective the women have a function in the story that limits their development as convincing characters.

The Adventures of Augie March is not an unqualified success, but it resolves some of the problems Bellow had with his earlier fiction. It opens up the narrative perspective, moving away from a closed and obsessive point of view. It abandons the tight, limiting structure of the earlier novels, seeking a form that is dictated by the material and accommodates it, rather than one that encloses its material in a preconceived aesthetic mould. It offers a vastly increased range of characters conceived in terms of their comic eccentricity. Most of all, it offers a new literary style, so distinctive that it has been called 'Bellovian', in the wonderful talking machine of Augie's voice that contains also the limitless polyphony of the world he inhabits.

Bellow's next important work is the novella *Seize the Day*. It was published in 1956 as part of a collection that included also three short stories, 'Looking for Mr. Green', 'The Gonzaga Manuscripts' and 'A Father-to-Be', and a play, *The Wrecker*, but it has in subsequent editions been issued without these other pieces. *Seize the Day* has as a central issue the oppression by money of the human spirit. It is a brief, concentrated piece that at first sight may seem to be a reversion to the mode of the forties novels. However, it lacks the claustrophobic atmosphere of those two books. The third-person narration broadens the perspective: at times we see things from the point of view of the protagonist, but we also see him as others see him, and the narrative voice itself usually remains at an ironic distance. In some ways, Tommy Wilhelm and his story seem to be a corrective to the uneasy optimism of *Augie March*. Wilhelm is ill-at-ease in himself and in the world he inhabits. He is not an appealing character. His body is large and clumsy, physically warped. He likes to wear good clothing, but his body distorts it into comic untidiness. His habits are slovenly: he is not very clean, using an electric shaver to avoid the need for water, his pockets are filled with crushed cigarette butts, and he uses the strings of red cellophane from cigarette packages as dental floss. He eats greedily in public places and drinks gin out of a coffee mug. His physical sloppiness supports an equivalent mental heaviness: he has a speech impediment that makes him inarticulate at times of emotion, and he sees his whole being as if it were a physical burden: 'The spirit, the peculiar burden of his existence lay upon him like an accretion, a load, a hump. In any moment of quiet, when sheer fatigue prevented him from struggling, he was apt to feel this mysterious weight, this growth or collection of nameless things which it was the business of his life to carry about' (Ch. 2). At times of extreme frustration with his burdensome being he calls himself a hippopotamus.

There is almost nothing in life that Wilhelm is able to cope with adequately, and his history is a series of perversely mistaken choices: 'After much thought and hesitation and debate he invariably took the course he had rejected innumerable times' (Ch. 1). He dropped out of college and went to Hollywood against the wishes of his parents, falsely persuaded by a transparently pathetic agent named Maurice Venice that he had talent as an actor, and remained there for seven years as an 'extra' (the word nicely suggests his sense of himself as a supernumerary person). He worked as a salesman for a company that sold children's furniture but quit when a son-in-law of one of the owners was promoted over him. His instability precipitated the breakdown of his marriage, and he is now estranged from his children and persecuted by his vindictive wife, Margaret, who constantly hounds him for money and will not give him a divorce. At the point where the novella begins he is gambling on the New York stock market in a last desperate attempt to make some money, but as with everything else, he is playing a game whose rules he does not understand. It is comically appropriate that he should have chosen to invest in lard, a thick, heavy rendering of pork fat.

Our laughter at Wilhelm's comic inadequacy is uncomfortable, however, because we are made aware that he suffers genuine pain and despair that arise out of his failure. Wilhelm believes in capitalism, but he lacks the qualities to succeed in the money world, at least as it is represented by New York. The true denizen of that world is Wilhelm's father, Dr Adler, and the ultimate source of Wilhelm's pain is his father's rejection of him. Wilhelm, in his mid-forties, still has a child's awe of this powerful, successful man, a child's fear of his anger, and an overwhelming need to be loved by him. Dr Adler, however, is fastidious, vain and cruel, and quite incapable of giving love – indeed, it is that very incapacity that has made him successful. His view of the world leaves no place for compassion; his rules are inflexible and make no allowance for human weakness, and so Wilhelm's suffering simply increases his anger and resentment. He is a fine representative of the drab, decaying New York that we encounter here, which seems to be a city of old men and women, like Mr Perls with his frazzle-face, his dyed hair and his mouth full of silver teeth, and Mr Rappaport, the blind old man who made his fortune out of killing chickens, who still comes daily in the hope of making a killing in the money market.

Seize the Day details the events of a single critical day in Wilhelm's life. He is temporarily living in the Hotel Gloriana, where his father also lives, and which is mainly inhabited by elderly people. On the morning of this day he takes breakfast with Dr Adler, from whom he hopes to get financial help, or at least some sign of sympathy, but receives nothing from him but selfish advice: 'Carry nobody on your back' (Ch. 3). He then goes for a second breakfast with Dr Tamkin, a psychologist-trickster who also lives in the Gloriana, and who seems to Wilhelm to be offering just the kind of support that Dr Adler refuses him. To this apparent surrogate father Wilhelm has entrusted his last seven hundred dollars in a joint investment, and the two go to a brokerage to see how their shares are doing, and then go to lunch. When Wilhelm returns to the brokerage after lunch he finds his investment wiped out. Unable to find Tamkin, he goes to his father to beg once more for help, and is flatly rejected. A phone call to his wife simply compounds his misery, because she is unrelenting in her demands for money. He wanders into the street, where there is a crowd in front of a funeral parlour. Swept into the chapel by the crowd of mourners, he gazes at the dead man there, and is overwhelmed by a wave of emotion that submerges self-pity in a generalized pity for mankind in what seems to be a transcendent vision.

The possible Oedipal elements in the painful relationship between Wilhelm and Dr Adler have inevitably led some critics to take a psychoanalytical approach to the novella. Some have gone beyond the Freudian model, seeing in Wilhelm's masochistic wallowing in grief and guilt, and in his feeling of physical and emotional constriction, a representation of the teachings on armouring of Wilhelm Reich, whose work Bellow was reading at the time when he wrote *Seize the Day*.[34] Reich's theories concern the ways in which the individual 'armours' himself in both body and character as a means of protecting himself against social and psychological circumstances, and certainly an understanding of this is helpful in explaining the novella's insistence on Wilhelm's sensation of choking and drowning as well as his constant attempts to hide or dissemble his feelings. An example of the physical expression of emotional pain comes when Wilhelm thinks of how his father is ashamed of him: 'He pressed his lips together and his tongue went soft; it pained him far at the back, in the cords and throat, and a knot of ill formed in his chest' (Ch. 1). Although his recognition of his father's unfairness sometimes fills him with rage, his problems do not arise from an Oedipal hatred of his father so much as from frustrated love, and Bellow is careful to relate Wilhelm's rejection by his father to his failure in the social and money world.

Dr Adler has succeeded because the sources of love have dried up in him. For him love is only self-love, generated by his admiration for his own success, and love and money have become identical, which is why he cannot respond to Wilhelm's pleas for help – he will not give him money, and therefore cannot give him love. This too is why he can only create an image of a lovable Wilhelm by fabricating a successful one whose income was 'up in the five figures'. Wilhelm sees this estrangement between father and son as being the pattern of the world, in which the economic potency of the one keeps the other immature. Thus, when he considers Mr Rappaport he thinks: 'this old man still makes money in the market. Is loaded with dough, probably. And I bet he doesn't give his children any. Some of them must be in their fifties. This is what keeps middle-aged men as children. He's master over the dough. Think – just think! Who controls everything? Old men of this type' (Ch. 6). This estrangement has put pressure on the integrity of Wilhelm's own identity; the sense of fragmentation is reflected in the multiplication of his names. His actual name is Wilhelm Adler, but he took the name 'Tommy Wilhelm' when he tried to break into the film world. The dropping of his surname represents a denial of his Jewish history, and his pseudonym implies a false persona that associates him with the Hollywood project of providing illusions for the defeated who, as defined by Maurice Venice, sound like Wilhelm himself: 'Listen, everywhere there are people trying hard, miserable, in trouble, downcast, tired, trying and trying. They need a break, right? A break through, a help, luck or sympathy' (Ch. 1). The fact that he has retained the name indicates his entrapment in this state of childish illusion; and his father's name for him, the apparently affectionate diminutive 'Wilky', actually conveys Dr Adler's contemptuous recognition of his childishness. Bewildered by the puzzle of who he really is, Wilhelm tries to understand Tamkin's account of the pretender soul, and goes back to the name 'Velvel' by which his grandfather had called him; this returns him to his Jewish origins, but it is still the name of a child.

Wilhelm's apparent inability to grow beyond a childish stage of development can, of course, be taken as the cause of the whole series of failures that constitute his life, and he may simply be seen, as his father sees him, as pathetically inadequate. But the book insists on equating his childishness not only with his need for love, but also with his need to *give* love. The failure of his marriage is not clearly explained, but what *is* clear is that conjugal love has turned into crushing materialism; he sees Margaret's efforts to squeeze money out of him as an attempt on his life: 'she's trying to put an end to me' (Ch. 3), he tells his father, and he says to her 'You must realize you're killing me' (Ch. 7). This may sound like melodramatic exaggeration, a distortion brought on by his self-pity, but the book makes only too clear how the pursuit of money can pervert natural affections or, as Tamkin has it, that there is no middle ground between 'construct' and 'destruct'.

It is Dr Tamkin who brings home to Wilhelm the connection between money-making and aggression, between the market and murder. Wilhelm himself has experienced this metaphor without understanding it, as he indicates when he thinks about his successful times: 'The money! When I had it, I flowed money. They bled it away from me. I haemorrhaged money' (Ch. 2). Tamkin builds a theory around this metaphor: 'People come to the market to kill.

They say, "I'm going to make a killing." It's not accidental. Only they haven't got the genuine courage to kill, and they erect a symbol of it. The money. They make a killing by a fantasy' (Ch. 4). This is one of the truths that Tamkin teaches Wilhelm almost by accident, for the irony here is that Tamkin himself is one of the market predators, a man who speculates with other people's money. Tamkin is a brilliant comic creation, a 'psychological poet' who spouts a philosophy derived from Emersonian self-reliance, an inventor of improbable devices and crazy notions, a fertile teller of stories, a 'confuser of the imagination' (Ch. 6). He is a charlatan, but his ability to improvise a story or idea that will supply a momentary need gives him a power over Wilhelm that is almost hypnotic. He acts as a surrogate father (the images of fathers carrying sons and sons carrying fathers recall Augie literally carrying his substitute father Einhorn in a figure of mutual obligation and dependence and have a poignant resonance in the light of Dr Adler's denial of any obligation to 'carry' his son) who seems to be offering Wilhelm comfort and concern that his own father will not provide. In the book's terms he too is a failure, because he embodies the very disease that he explains, and yet from his teachings Wilhelm is able to take some ideas that he recognizes as truths, not least the injunction to find his true self, and to 'seize the day'.

The well-known phrase that stands as title of this novella offers an instructive ambiguity. It is a translation of a Latin phrase, *carpe diem*, first used by the poet Horace, and generally applied to a kind of literature, usually lyric poetry, that encourages a materialistic enjoyment of the present moment on the grounds that life is short. In sixteenth- and seventeenth-century English love poetry it became part of a seducer's persuasions of his mistress; probably the best-known version of it comes in the first lines of a poem by Robert Herrick, 'To the Virgins, to Make Much of Time':

Gather ye rosebuds while ye may,
Old Time is still a-flying. . . .

Paradoxically, however, although the injunction to 'seize the day' appears to promote immediate self-gratification (which is how Tamkin intends it), its effect is usually to provoke a consideration of the chilling inevitability of diminishment and death, and it is to this that Wilhelm is led at the end of the story.

Whether or not Wilhelm learns anything from the truths he recognizes is arguable. The injunction to him in Tamkin's poem to know and value himself is good advice (though not, perhaps, as Tamkin himself understands it), and if Wilhelm were to take it he would get out of the market and out of the city. Through a complex set of allusions and memories the narrative hints at the possibility of a simpler, peaceful life that might be called, for want of a better term, 'pastoral'. On the most immediate level this is reflected in Wilhelm's desire, fed by memories of the apartment he once had in Roxbury, to escape from the weight of city life to the country. It is reflected too in his nostalgia for times in the past when he was loved, by his grandfather, by his long-dead mother, even by Margaret before their marriage went sour. More obliquely, it comes from the fragments of poems about escape or removal to a better world or higher state that keep surfacing in his mind: Keats's *Endymion*, Yeats's 'Sailing to Byzantium', Milton's 'Lycidas'. Of course, there is some irony in all of this, for it is clear that Wilhelm's memory has idealized those peaceful moments of the past – as the narrative voice points out about his longing for Roxbury, 'he forgot that that time had had its troubles, too' (Ch. 3) – and his understanding of the poems he remembers seems vague, a sentimental response to the emotional power of the words. Still, these pastoral intimations do associate him with values that are fundamentally opposed to the arid values of the marketplace.

Indeed, in spite of his self-pity, Wilhelm is a man of good will, able to find compassion for his father who, constantly aware of the closeness of death, still clings to all he has and can find nothing but resentment for his son who will go on living after his death. It is this that gives Wilhelm credibility as a hero, and we must bear it in mind when considering the novella's conclusion. As with Bellow's earlier novels, the ending of *Seize the Day* has called up conflicting responses; as Harvey Swados put it in his review, the book 'culminates in an extraordinary ending which is going to be read and argued over for a long time to come'.[35] Is Wilhelm's flood of tears in the funeral parlour an extreme manifestation of his self-pity, or is it a sign of a saving insight? Are we to see in it failure or catharsis?[36] The question can best be considered in relation to the imagery of water that pervades the story.

The novella presents a sustained pattern of water-related images, from the opening paragraph, in which Wilhelm sinks and sinks in the elevator to the lobby with its billowing carpet and drapes like sails, to the closing paragraph where he sinks, once again, in the 'sea-like music' of the funeral chapel. The water imagery here holds out conflicting possibilities. One is that water is a destructive element, and certainly the frequent images of descent and immersion coupled with Wilhelm's sensation of choking imply that he is drowning. But water is also the medium of baptism, of cleansing. The great flood of tears in which he sinks, therefore, could indicate a suicidal drowning in self-pity, or it could be that he sheds tears of compassion and understanding for the inevitable end of all men that he confronts in the dead man: 'the sea-like music came up to his ears. It poured into him where he had hidden himself in the centre of a crowd by the great and happy oblivion of tears. He heard it and sank deeper than sorrow, through torn sobs and cries toward the consummation of his heart's ultimate need'. Perhaps the implications of 'deeper than sorrow' and 'the con-summation of his heart's ultimate need' are too imprecise for us to understand them as indicating any triumph, and, unlike Lycidas who, 'sunk ... beneath the wat'ry floor', will rise in triumph, Wilhelm will still have to face the troubles that 'drowned' him, because they have not gone away.

Wilhelm is a failure in the world presented in the novel, a world in which he believes, and in which he desperately wants to succeed. He is misguided in this, but we can sympathize with him because those who succeed in this world are like his father, unable to respond to or with human feeling. Wilhelm does have such feeling, however repressed it may sometimes seem, and is to be valued for that. This is what distinguishes his self-pity from his father's: Wilhelm's does not exclude pity for those outside himself, and that is a small victory.

Early in 1959 an essay by Bellow appeared in the *New York Times Book Review* warning 'deep readers' against looking too eagerly in fictions for symbolic meanings that might lead them astray.[37] Bellow may have written with tongue in cheek, for in that same year he published *Henderson the Rain King*; of all his novels this is the one that offers the most temptation to deep readers (if there *is* an element of jest here it may be a part of the same joke that the hero's first wife, who receives little sympathy in the book, is described as 'a very deep reader'). Henderson does not move in Bellow's familiar urban landscape of Chicago or New York, but is placed instead in Africa. This is not an Africa that anyone might visit, however, but one constructed out of Bellow's fancy, and out

of his reading of works of travellers in Africa such as Sir Richard
Burton's *First Footsteps in East Africa*, and of anthropologists like his
one-time teacher Melville J. Herskovitz, who studied cattle-raising
tribes in Africa.[38] Bellow was not much concerned with accuracy
here, and his Africa is very much a place of the imagination, built
on a framework of fertility myth, and with a wide range of Biblical,
literary and cultural allusion that gives it an extraordinary sugges-
tiveness and resonance. Thus the story has the dream-like quality
of romance, a quality that Henderson himself brings to the reader's
attention on more than one occasion: 'not the least of the difficulties is that it happened as in a dream' (Ch. 3).

The elderly, twice-married millionaire Eugene Henderson may
seem an odd choice for a hero. He is eccentric, physically large and
powerful and prone to apparently irrational violence. His appearance is comic, bordering on the grotesque. He is profoundly
alienated from the meaningless materialism of his life in post-war
America. Driven by a vision of his existence as a piling-up of 'junk',
by profound feelings of guilt, and by an unsilenceable inner voice
that says only 'I want!' and will not let him rest, he journeys to
Africa. With Romilayu, an African guide whose firmly-held Christian beliefs offer a quiet spiritual message to the driven Henderson,
he goes on a quest that is not clearly defined, since the driving voice
will not say what it wants, but one of the things he seeks is a
justification of his individual existence through the performance of
an act that only he can do. He first visits the Arnewi, a tribe of
gentle, cattle-worshipping people who are suffering from a
drought and a water supply polluted with frogs. He sees here an
opportunity to prove himself by applying Western technology to
the problem, but the bomb he makes to destroy the frogs blows up
the reservoir, and he leaves in shame. He moves on to the Wariri, a
cruel, aggressive and devious people, and befriends their enigmatic
king, Dahfu. The Wariri rain-making ceremony gives him a second
chance to prove himself uniquely useful when his prodigious
strength enables him to lift their idol Mummah and bring on the
rains, and for this he is appointed Sungo, or Rain King. He
becomes the pupil of Dahfu, who tries, with limited success, to instil
in him some of the properties of Atti, his pet lioness, and he
accompanies Dahfu on a hunt for another lion, Gmilo, which is
believed by the Wariri to be the reincarnation of Dahfu's father.
Dahfu is killed by the lion he has trapped, and Henderson,
understanding that he is to replace Dahfu as king, flees with a lion

cub containing the spirit of Dahfu and returns to America. The improbability of this narrative is irrelevant, because Bellow is rewriting the modern romantic myth of the individual escaping from civilization to seek fundamental truths through a confrontation with the wilderness. In its exploration of the dangerously ambivalent attractions that Africa has for the Western mind *Henderson the Rain King* has affinities with Conrad's *Heart of Darkness*. It also reworks a central theme of American literature, memorably expressed in Huck Finn's decision to eschew 'civilisation' and 'light out for the territory', which emerges in the distinctively American code of romantic heroism associated particularly with Ernest Hemingway, an attitude that seeks to overcome fear of annihilation by confronting death in its most savage aspects. Henderson himself (his initials give the joke away) can be taken as a burlesque evocation of Hemingway's code of masculine bravado.[39] The American myth of escape, in its twentieth-century manifestation, is related to the larger concern of literary modernism with a vision of contemporary Western society as a spiritual desert, a vision that found its quintessential expression in the poetry of T. S. Eliot. Eliot's sterile Waste Land is vainly awaiting the arrival of the hero who will revive it with healing waters; the would-be hero Henderson is all too successful in his endeavours to bring water to the African tribes.

These are serious ideas and Bellow himself treated them seriously in his own earlier fictions, dealing with the struggle of the alienated man to find meaning in his life. Here, however, they seem to be subverted by the comic treatment: the Hemingway hero becomes ludicrous when embodied in the undignified figure of Henderson, and Henderson himself deals irreverently with the enervated plaint of the nightingale in Eliot's 'Burnt Norton' that human kind cannot stand very much reality: 'But how much unreality can it stand? ... I fired that question right back at the nightingale. So what if reality may be terrible? It's better than what we've got' (Ch. 9). The comic treatment has disturbed some critics: Tanner, for example, worried that 'profound notions seem to flirt with their own parodies and a genuine seriousness of inquiry is jostled and tripped by the immense comic gusto which hurtles the book along'.[40] However, this division between the serious and the parodic seems to correspond to a division in Henderson himself, between on the one hand the aspiring spirit that tries to reach the dead through music, to discover reality, to learn how to confront

death, and on the other the earth-bound body, moving insistently
downward into farce. The implications of this division are addres-
sed by Dahfu's psychosomatic theories.

The novel's 'comic gusto' is generated by a narrative voice that
contains an energy that is distinctive even in comparison with the
voice of Augie March. Eugene Henderson is Bellow's first non-
Jewish protagonist and the first to have inherited a place at the
centre of American wealth, power and culture. From one point of
view he may seem to be an extreme development of the figure of
the aggressive, drunken, self-destructive white Anglo-Saxon, a
version of Kirby Allbee. He nevertheless has much in common with
Bellow's earlier Jewish heroes, particularly in his sense of himself as
an outsider (like Asa Leventhal he feels that he occupies a place
that belongs to someone else); he has especially strong similarities
to that other large, clumsy sufferer, Tommy Wilhelm. In Henderson's opening statement about himself, in which he lays claim to a
larger-than-life grief that translates itself into physical suffering, he
echoes Wilhelm. The voice is different, however. Henderson
presents a synopsis of his life through an extreme version of the
kind of Witmanesque catalogue that Bellow developed for Augie
March:

> When I think of my condition at the age of fifty-five … all is
> grief. The facts begin to crowd me and soon I get a pressure in
> the chest. A disorderly rush begins – my parents, my wives, my
> girls, my children, my farm, my animals, my habits, my money,
> my music lessons, my drunkenness, my prejudices, my brutality,
> my teeth, my face, my soul! I have to cry, 'No, no, get back, curse
> you, let me alone!' But how can they let me alone? They are
> mine. And they pile into me from all sides. It turns into chaos.

Along with other things that are parodied in this novel Bellow
includes his own writing style.

Tommy Wilhelm suffered from his inability to survive in the
money world. The wealthy Henderson has all the things that
Wilhelm aspired to, yet he too is suffocating, drowning in the
money world, and his economic freedom has ironically generated
in him a sense of his own uselessness. His inarticulate frustration
has manifested itself in careless and destructive treatment of his
family and a conscious refusal of socially acceptable behaviour.
Indeed, he inverts the social aspiration that we saw in Wilhelm, for

although he attended an Ivy League university and has a Master's degree he makes an effort to appear an ignorant slob. His conversion of his family estate into a home for pigs is simply the most spectacular of his gestures of defiance of social decencies. Henderson does recognize in himself the need for something higher, however, for some spiritual nourishment, and it is this that motivates his attempts to reach his dead father through his violin.

The broken relationship with the father is a recurring motif in Bellow's fifties novels. Augie's father was conveniently and anonymously absent, allowing the March brothers to build fictions around him, but much of the motivation of Augie's story is his search for a substitute father as a source of love and authority. Dr Adler's refusal to give his son love or any other kind of help is at the centre of Wilhelm's problems. Henderson believes that his father resented him for being alive after the accidental death of his brother. What this repeated pattern seems to imply is a dislocation from the past, a separation from sources of loving authority, a sense of the failure of history to provide truths or answers. In Henderson's case this is reflected in his recognition of the ambiguity underlying the foundations of his own family's wealth: his ancestors were nation builders, but they were also dishonest manipulators – that, indeed, was a necessary condition for their success. It is this recognition, perhaps, that urges him to trample down the material evidence of success. There is a pleasing irony in the story Henderson tells of his search through his father's books to find the source of a quotation about the forgiveness of sins, a search that turned up only the banknotes his father had used as bookmarks, only material answers to spiritual questions.

Henderson is a symptom of the culture he inhabits. American economic optimism had in the post-war years generated a gross materialism, something weighed down by itself, just as Henderson is weighed down by the material bulk of his own body. Much of the novel's comedy is farce, dependent on the gigantic joke of Henderson's corporeal being, of which he constantly reminds us, in a self-mocking way. He is the victim of haemorrhoids and crab-lice, he suffers from the disaster of his broken bridge-work, the indignity of his unwashed jockey-shorts and of his great body wrapped in the transparent Sungo drawers. But the body that is subject to such comic indignity is subject also to the tragic indignity of death. At 55 an increasing awareness of his mortality has inflated Henderson's desire to find a meaning for his life into frenzied proportions. His decision to go to Africa arises from a need to escape from his constricting self and from the mass of material things. It is precipitated by a flash of insight that he experiences when he goes into the cottage of his home-help Miss Lenox, whose death he has just inadvertently caused, and finds mountains of useless objects, the collection of a lifetime that actually *defines* that life. He thinks:

> Why do we allow ourselves? What are we doing? The last little room of dirt is waiting. Without windows. So for God's sake make a move, Henderson, put forth effort. You, too, will die of this pestilence. Death will annihilate you and nothing will remain, and there will be nothing left but junk.   (Ch. 4)

This vision of a junk-culture is also a vision of Henderson's own spiritual condition, as is indicated later in a conversation he has with the Arnewi prince Itelo: 'My soul is like a pawn shop. I mean it's filled with unredeemed pleasures, old clarinets, and cameras, and moth-eaten fur' (Ch. 7). So Henderson takes flight from it.

Henderson's anxieties drive him out to Africa and, in a sense, back through history, beyond the roots of civilization, looking for answers. His problem is that he does not really know what the question is and the inner voice that says 'I want' won't tell him. What he is seeking has much to do with death, as represented by his recurring memory of the octopus in the aquarium at Banyules, but it has also to do with a need to find a use for himself, as expressed in his ambition to qualify as a doctor. He needs to find a reality beyond the ego-emphasizing idea of 'It's you who makes the world what it is. Reality is *you*' (Ch. 10), but the closest he can come to articulating his need is in vague ideas about the difference between 'becoming' and 'being', and bursting the spirit's sleep. What does emerge from this, however, is a powerful sense of urgency, of time running out.

The two tribes Henderson meets in Africa offer him opposed responses to experience. The Arnewi are a gentle, passive people who accept whatever befalls them with patience, while the Wariri are violent and aggressive, determined to impose their will on the world to the extent of beating and dominating their gods. In their own language the two tribes define the difference between them in terms of luck, but this implies that they have no control over what happens to them. The Arnewi, however, are acquiescent victims of their own beliefs, of fate, of natural circumstances and, eventually, of Henderson. Cattle worshippers who depend on water, they are suffering from a drought and a water supply that is contaminated with frogs. Their religion will not allow them to use polluted water, but it will not let them harm the frogs either. They must, therefore, suffer, but it is not simply a matter of bad luck. The 'lucky' Wariri are not in fact prepared to trust to luck; they manipulate their religion and dominate one another through trickery or violence to get the results they want. The difference is between passive acquiescence and willed seizing of control, something like the difference between Augie and the Machiavellians or Wilhelm and Dr Adler. It is a difference that might also be seen in terms of the conventional distinctions between feminine and masculine.

The gentleness of the Arnewi finds its highest form in their queen, Willatale, and Henderson is deeply attracted by it. When he arrives at the Arnewi village he thinks that it looks very old, and this suggests to him that he has arrived at a source of truth and life. He says to Romilayu, ' "Hell, it looks like the original place. It must be older than the city of Ur." Even the dust had a flavour of great age, I thought' (Ch.5). 'The original place' suggests paradise, but what Henderson learns amongst the Arnewi is that a place of innocence might be the opposite of a paradise, for their gentle passivity simply ensures that the Arnewi will suffer constantly. Still, they do offer some truth to Henderson, for they have refined acceptance of suffering into a principle that they term 'Bittahness'. This takes its highest form in their queen, Willatale, who lives life with absolute serenity. The advice she offers Henderson, 'Grun-tu-molani. Man want to live' (Ch. 7), seems to him to be profoundly true, for it was his burning rage to live rather than simply to exist that drove him out on his quest. But Henderson still does not know how to 'want to live' in the right way, and his desire to be of assistance destroys his chance to learn more from the Arnewi when he destroys their reservoir.

The implied answer is that, properly to live, a man must come to terms with death, and this is what Henderson has been fleeing. Willatale's serenity arises from her acceptance of the inevitability of death, as symbolized by the lion skin she wears, though Henderson does not yet realize this: 'Had I known then what I know now about lions, this would have told me much about her' (Ch. 7). When he arrives amongst the Wariri Henderson finds himself surrounded by reminders of death: hanging bodies, the corpse in his hut, a shrunken head, the skulls with which Dahfu plays. The Wariri are cruel and violent, determined to impose their will upon the world (it is their flogging of their gods that particularly upsets Henderson), but ironically their society seems to Henderson much more 'modern' than the Arnewi society. Their town is better built and planned, they have a bureaucracy and a police force, they have modern weapons, and their politics are devious.

It is the Wariri king, Dahfu, who becomes Henderson's real teacher. In some ways Dahfu is much like Henderson. Within his own society he is a misfit, 'the only occupant of a certain class' (Ch. 17), as Henderson puts it. He has kept the lioness Atti in defiance of the will of his people, as Henderson kept his pigs as a gesture of social defiance. The questions that interest him are the questions that interest Henderson. Unlike Henderson, however, he is at ease with himself and apparently at ease with the world, physically and spiritually noble, and Henderson takes him as a visionary who might be a saviour. But Dahfu is not to be taken completely seriously, because he is also in part a reworking of Dr Tamkin, a persuasive crank who gives the impression of having the answers. His teachings, like Tamkin's, have their source in the work of Wilhelm Reich. They are based on psychosomatic theories of disease, which argue that some physical diseases have mental causes. Dahfu goes much further in his concern with the dynamic relations between mind and body and the ways in which these can transform each other: 'The spirit of the person in a sense is the author of his body' (Ch. 17), he says, and he sees the individual as a kind of artist, whose main work of art is his body. If this is true, it seems to Henderson, it has terrible implications about the mind that created the great ruin that is *his* body: 'For if I was the painter of my own nose and forehead and of such a burly stoop and such arms and fingers, why, it was an out-and-out felony against myself' (Ch. 18).

This is why Henderson reluctantly submits himself to Dahfu's experiment. Dahfu claims that his own powers are generated by his contact with the lion, and to unmake and remake himself Henderson must descend into the lion pit. By imitating the beast, by taking on certain of its physical properties or manners, Henderson can develop something of its spirit. Henderson is highly sceptical about Dahfu's theories, but he follows him into the lion's den because he is carried away by his affirmation, and in spite of his fear he does not wish to lose Dahfu's respect. But in confronting the lioness he is not learning the qualities that Dahfu intends him to learn. He roars like the lion not because he is trying to emulate it, but because he is terrified. Still, somehow he does learn something from his ordeal: 'I had a voice that said, *I* want! *I* want? It should have told me *she* wants, *he* wants, *they* want. And moreover, it's love that makes reality reality. The opposite makes the opposite' (Ch. 19). And he sees through his own ego-emphasis and self-pity.

Henderson's belief that he now knows what it is that constitutes reality is ill-founded, however. The climax of the novel comes with Dahfu's disastrous attempt to capture the lion that contains the spirit of his father. Moments before Dahfu's fall Henderson looks into the lion's face, the face of death, and finds that reality offers more terror than he had ever imagined. This lion, angry and threatening death, is vastly different from the tame Atti, and Henderson thinks: 'The snarling of this animal was indeed the voice of death. And I thought how I had boasted to my dear Lily how I loved reality. ... But oh, unreality! Unreality, unreality! That had been my scheme for a troubled but eternal life' (Ch. 20). This is the moment of fullest vision for Henderson, when he comes face to face with the things he has always avoided. And so, in spite of his terror, he is able to throw himself on to the lion and bind it in an attempt to save his friend, the nobility of his instinct being greater than his fear.

We are intended to see elements of spiritual regeneration here, and they are underlined by Henderson's burial and symbolic resurrection. He is locked into the tomb in which the body of Dahfu is laid, and there is a moment of identification with his dead friend: 'As I had tried to stop his bleeding, there was blood all over me and soon it was dry. I tried to rub it off. Well, I thought, maybe this is a sign that I should continue his existence?' (Ch. 21). Accordingly, Henderson rises from the grave carrying the lion cub that supposedly contains the spirit of Dahfu. He makes his escape from the Wariri and flies back to America with whatever lesson he has learned. The novel leaves us with a final euphoric image: Henderson's plane has landed for fuel in Newfoundland, and we see him joyfully running around it in the snow, carrying the cub and an orphan child who is travelling alone to America, 'leaping, leaping, pounding, and tingling over the pure white lining of the grey Arctic silence'.

How are we to understand this ending? Like the endings of all Bellow's earlier novels, it has come in for its share of criticism.

There have been complaints that Henderson's return to America is anti-climactic after the extraordinary experiences he has undergone, and others that the novel is incomplete or evasive because it does not show what happens to Henderson after his return. Both criticisms imply that *Henderson the Rain King* does not adequately resolve the aesthetic and ethical tensions that its narrative has set up. In his review of the novel when it first appeared Norman Podhoretz articulated a view that many have echoed: 'the note of affirmation on which Mr. Bellow closes is not in the least convincing, and altogether lacks the force to counteract the magnificent passages of anguish and despair that fill the body of the book.'[41] Podhoretz means that the positive ending is unearned, that we do not believe that Henderson's experiences could have led him to the apparent optimism that it suggests. This may be a result of 'the familiar formal problem of a novelist whose subject is the comic spiritual seeker'.[42] It has exercised so many critics that it has to be given serious consideration.

Part of the problem may be an effect of the shifting meaning that the book attaches to the word 'reality', and the imprecise definition of what it is that Henderson is seeking, a problem helped not at all by the fact that Henderson seeks reality in a totally unrealistic landscape. But Henderson himself believes that his ordeal has taught him something, as he says at the outset of his story: 'the world which I thought so mighty an oppressor has removed its wrath from me'. Perhaps we could say that he has earned his lion skin; he has faced death and recognized its power, and in doing so he has understood that the serene happiness of Bittahness is only possible with this insight, which is also 'reality'. But this recognition is also presented as part of a child-like state (that of the innocent Arnewi), and this too is implied in the novel's conclusion. In describing the orphan on the plane Henderson says: 'he was still trailing his clc d of glory. God knows, I dragged mine as long as I could till it got dingy, mere tatters of grey fog. However, I always knew what it was' (Ch. 22). The reference here is to William Wordsworth's 'Immortality Ode', a poem that mystifies the innocence of the child as a superior intuitive understanding and proclaims the importance of memory for the adult who wishes to resist his progressive separation from nature. It is surely significant that while sitting on the plane with the child and the cub, Henderson moves backwards through memory to his own youth and the crucial moment of estrangement from his father. In this he finds no consolation, but his memory also returns to him a long-forgotten moment of love in which he *does* find consolation, in the story of his fairground job riding a roller-coaster with the ruined old bear Smolak, and of how the two comforted each other in their pain. This wonderful story is both comic and moving, and from it Henderson learns that 'for creatures there is nothing that ever runs unmingled' (Ch. 22). It is a fitting ending to the novel, and it points us forward to a preoccupation that became increasingly important in the novels that followed this one: the complex integrative processes of memory.

4

Novels of the Sixties and Seventies

The sixties and seventies were the peak years of Bellow's career. As far as fiction is concerned, he produced only three novels and a number of short stories, some of these collected in *Mosby's Memoirs and Other Stories* (1968), but the general critical consensus would place *Herzog* (1964), *Mr. Sammler's Planet* (1970) and *Humboldt's Gift* (1975) at the centre of his literary achievement. His interests moved him in a number of other directions, too: he was, briefly, co-editor of a literary journal called *The Noble Savage*; he made his abortive forays into the theatre with *The Last Analysis* and his three one-act plays; and his increasing activity as social, cultural and political commentator led him into journalism and, eventually, the writing of *To Jerusalem and Back* (1976).

The Last Analysis was written while Bellow was working on *Herzog*, and it merits brief consideration here. The play's 1964 theatrical failure may have resulted in part from the fact that Bellow, whose constant re-writing and refinement of his fiction demonstrates a need for absolute control over his material, was ill at ease with a collaborative medium in which he could not have the last word. But in its final version, which the author revised for publication, *The Last Analysis* is a funny and intelligent play, a farcical spoof of Freudian psychoanalysis. While its protagonist is foolish, we can sympathize with him because of his honest intentions; he is a more ridiculous Henderson, akin also to Herzog. The play's central issue, as defined by Bellow himself in a note attached to the published version, relates it to a fundamental preoccupation of most of his subsequent fiction, 'the mind's comical struggle for survival in an environment of Ideas'.[43] The disaster of *The Last Analysis* must have pained Bellow; but his experience in the theatre provided material for *Humboldt's Gift*, his failure therapeutically transformed into Charlie Citrine's great critical and commercial triumph.

Herzog appeared in the same year as *The Last Analysis*, and it was welcomed by many reviewers as the masterpiece that Bellow had long been expected to produce. To one reviewer it was a 'well-nigh faultless novel', to another it was 'a great comic novel' that could be favourably compared with Joyce's *Ulysses*.[44] Perhaps *Herzog* gave the impression of being a masterpiece because it could so clearly be seen as the culmination of a line of development taken by the earlier novels: its protagonist is a larger, more intellectual version of the alienated 'dangling' man trying to survive in the modern urban jungle, the Jewish inheritor (and victim) of Western culture looking for meaning in contemporary urban life. The novel achieves a fusion of the dark, enclosed atmosphere of Bellow's shorter fictions with the expansive energy of his longer novels. David Galloway suggested that Bellow had, in effect, only written one book from six different points of view, with *Herzog* as the final variation of them.[45] This, however, does not indicate the superior refinement of *Herzog*, and it might be truer to say that each of Bellow's novels developed out of the one before it; Bellow himself seems to have seen something of this, for he has said of *Herzog*, 'I felt I was completing a certain development, coming to the end of a literary situation'.[46]

Praise of *Herzog* was not by any means unanimous. In a violent attack in *Partisan Review* Richard Poirier condemned the book as a pretentious failure, its perspective made incoherent by the impossibility of separating Herzog from his creator: 'What is missing is any indication that Bellow is aware of the *essential* irrelevance, the *essential* pretension and shabbiness of the self-aggrandizing mind at work in, and for, the hero'.[47] John Aldridge echoed the accusation that the novel smugly aggrandizes its protagonist, and argued that it had been accepted as a major work by the intellectual community largely because it gave them a justification for their sense of superiority.[48] A common response from the more judicious reviewers, such as Irving Howe, was to acknowledge the achievement of the novel while noting its flaws: 'In the end one feels that *Herzog* is too hermetic a work, the result of a technique which encloses us rigidly in the troubles of a man during his phase of withdrawal from the world. The material is absorbing in its own right; it is handled with great skill; but in relation to the intended theme, it all seems a little puny'.[49]

By the mid-sixties Bellow had established his reputation as the most intelligent novelist of his generation, and each of the novels he had produced over the preceding twenty years had had its champions. *Herzog* appeared to proclaim itself a masterpiece by being quintessential Bellow, by subsuming in itself the merits of the earlier fictions while transcending their limitations. It is interesting to note, however, that the major reservation underlying the criticisms of Poirier, Aldridge and Howe concerns the novel's perspective, the problematical relationship between author, narrating voice, and character. As with earlier novels, a question is raised about how we are to judge the experience of the protagonist and, more to the point, how we are to judge the protagonist's response to his experience; and this raises the further question of whether the optimism of the ending is justified by that experience. The limitations that these critics perceived, in other words, are limitations that were perceived also in the earlier novels.

In *Dangling Man, The Adventures of Augie March* and *Henderson the Rain King* the narrative voice is that of the protagonist himself. There is no external voice to provide an alternative perspective or point of judgement. The reader consequently has a difficult task in deciding how much ironic distance there is between the author's intention and the narrating voice. In *The Victim* Asa Leventhal is presented by a third-person narrator, which generates a greater sense of distance, but even there the point of view is most of the time Leventhal's own. The narrative voice of *Seize the Day* moves in and out of Tommy Wilhelm's mind, but generally it encloses the reader within Wilhelm's consciousness. In each of these cases it is probable that Bellow is intentionally exploiting ambiguity, for he is dealing with a mind that sees from a perspective that is in some degree distorted; the *intended* effect of the narrative position is to make it difficult to be precise about the limits of the distortion. This is, obviously, a risky device, since it leaves Bellow open to the kind of critical charge that we have seen.

Bellow makes his intentions plain in *Herzog* in the novel's celebrated opening sentence: 'If I am out of my mind, it's all right with me, thought Moses Herzog'. We are immediately made aware that Herzog is in an unusual state of mind, and offered the possibility that he is insane, but the 'if' prevents us from taking it as a certainty. Herzog's view that being out of his mind is 'all right' complicates the issue: in what circumstances would it be all right to be insane? The answer would seem to depend upon who it is that has defined the insanity; the novel goes on: 'Some people thought he was cracked and for a time he himself had doubted that he was all there. But now, though he still behaved oddly, he felt confident, cheerful, clairvoyant and strong'. Herzog is not mad, but he is in an aberrant state (later we discover that he has exhibited all the symptoms of paranoia); like the madness of Hamlet, however (with whom Herzog has been compared), its nature and boundaries are difficult to assess. The difficulty is compounded by the shiftiness of the narrative voice, which frequently slides from third to first person (a device with which Bellow was increasingly comfortable). This further confuses the status of the narrative: 'Ah, poor fellow! – and Herzog momentarily joined the objective world in looking down on himself. He too could smile at Herzog and despise him. But there still remained the fact. *I* am Herzog. I have to *be* that man. There is no one else to do it' (Ch. 3). It is this blurring of the distinction between first and third person that provides the ground for criticisms like Howe's, that the reader is too rigidly enclosed within Herzog, or worse, for the charges of Poirier and Aldridge that what they see as Herzog's smug self-satisfaction is somehow Bellow's own.

The charge that Bellow has failed sufficiently to detach himself from his creation has a further basis. In most of the novels prior to *Herzog* there is an autobiographical element, but in *Herzog* and the series of novels that follow it this element is vastly increased. Here, the lengthy account of Herzog's background, of his immigrant family and his childhood in Montreal, is fairly closely based on Bellow's own childhood, and this section bears a strong emotional weight. Herzog's two divorces and their bitter aftermath, as well as his victimization by lawyers, have their source in Bellow's recent experience. The temptation of critics to see in Bellow's later narrators a mouthpiece for the author has obviously been great. In his interview with Jo Brans Bellow gave an account of Herzog that suggested that he believed he had provided a way of looking objectively at the character, through Herzog's own recognition of his pretension. There is in Herzog, he said, 'a kind of self-critical comic sense, an amused objectivity toward himself, almost amounting to courage. . . . I think of him as a man who, in the agony of suffering, finds himself to be his own most penetrating critic. And he re-examines his life, as it were, by re-enacting all the roles he took seriously.' Herzog, 'that suffering joker', has an ironic self-awareness that allows him to be objective about himself, but it is matched by an inability to be objective about those who, like his ex-wife Madeleine or his one-time friend Valentine, he thinks have harmed him, for 'he's at war and he can't be fair'.[50] What critics like Poirier took to be confusion is complexity, a density of form that demands a very alert response from its reader, and for that Bellow has no need to apologize.

The state of Herzog's mind, then, makes up the texture of the book, and the looseness of structure in the organization of the material into nine unnumbered chapters mimics the groping of his mind towards meaning. The novel's opening sentence is actually a thought that he has almost at the end of the story (it is repeated in the final chapter); the acceptance of his situation, the movement towards equilibrium implied in it, is something that in the course of the novel he has had to work for. From this point of near-equilibrium the novel circles back through Herzog's thoughts over the events of the past few days, but takes in much of the experience of his entire life, as well as the materials of his intellectual furnishings. The novel is, in effect, an act of Herzog's memory (it is worth noting that memory becomes increasingly important in *Herzog* and the novels following it); it is not a writing so much as a re-writing of his history. And if we see history not as a set of facts but as a process of interpretation, then we can also see memory as akin to imagination a faculty that reorders or edits experience to give it shape and meaning. There are subjective truths, that is, but relating them to objective 'truth' is deeply problematical.

The events of the novel are easily described. Moses E. Herzog, a professor teaching in New York who specializes in the history of culture, is at his dilapidated country-house in Ludeyville, Massachusetts trying to recover from his divorce from his second wife, Madeleine, who is living in Chicago with their daughter June and Valentine Gersbach, once Herzog's best friend. Herzog considers the events of the past few days that have led him to this place. They began with his attempt to avoid the emotional pressure put on him by his mistress Ramona Donsell; he fled to the home of a friend in Vineyard Haven, but found himself too disturbed to remain there, so he returned to New York and spent a night with Ramona. On the following day he visited the courthouse to meet his lawyer, Harvey Simkin. While he was there, however, he overheard a court case in which a young man and woman were being tried for the murder of the woman's child, and this generated in him a sudden fear for the safety of his own child. He flew to Chicago and, overwhelmed by an urge to kill Madeleine and Gersbach, visited the home of his stepmother, where he picked up his late father's pistol, and went to Madeleine's house. His murderous urge left him when, looking through a bathroom window, he saw Gersbach bathing June and suddenly realized the comic absurdity of his situation. On the following morning he arranged to take June to a museum and aquarium, but got involved in a collision, and when the police arrived he was booked for carrying the gun. Released with the aid of his brother Will, he retired to the Ludeyville house, and this is the point where the novel begins.

Herzog, scholar and womanizer, is working in the rarefied atmosphere of the intellectual uplands. He is doing, as he puts it, 'the work of the future' (Ch. 4), counteracting the banalities of mass man; upon this project, as he sees it, depends the survival of civilization. He is super-sensitive, a great sufferer who thinks he has been unfairly knocked about by the world, betrayed by those he has loved. Like Henderson, he views the chaos of his personal life as a matter of his misplacement within contemporary history, and like Henderson he sets out on an exploration of the meaning of his time and his own place within it. But whereas Henderson hurls himself into a physical journey, a wandering that takes him to a confrontation with a mythicized version of the world, Herzog's wandering takes place within himself, through his own past, and also through theories and ideas that purport to explain the meaning of history. The events of the novel are really only a framework upon which Bellow has hung the important action, which is the flux of Herzog's mind. In his spiritual and mental turmoil he writes letters, which are never sent, to relatives, friends, mistresses, philosophers, historians, politicians, to the dead as well as the living, finally even to God. All his thoughts and preoccupations about his past, about his marriages and his other relationships, as well as his concerns about history and contemporary civilization, are exposed in these letters and in flashbacks and meditations relating to them. The novel's real action is Herzog's frenzied re-examination of his total experience, his attempt to give order and meaning to his life.

Through Herzog's letters Bellow is able to present a far wider range of intellectual reference than was possible in his earlier novels, allowing a clear sense of a powerful intelligence at work. Herzog himself is a historian, with a particular interest in the roots of Romanticism, and by interweaving Herzog's cultural ideas with his concern about his own experience, Bellow is able to imply an equation between Herzog's history and contemporary history. The Jewish intellectual, uprooted and spiritually dislocated into the chaos of contemporary American materialism (or, as Herzog has it, the dreamer cleaned out by sharpies) becomes for the author an instrument for measuring the decay of love in the modern world. Herzog, then, is a hero for what Bellow sees as a time of intellectual crisis. The aim of Herzog's own intellectual work is no less than a complete history of the twentieth century, an ambitious project that will give the modern moment an account of itself, explain its fragmentation. He sees cultural fragmentation as deriving partly from a decay of personal relations; his own sense of personal isolation arises from the failure of his own relationships, but he considers his failure within a context of theories and explanations derived from the main impulses of contemporary thought. He sees himself as the representative of love, of 'heart', as his name implies; he is a 'throb-hearted character' (Ch. 9), threatened by 'sharpies', realists or 'Reality Instructors' like his lawyer-friend Sandor Himmelstein, who want to show him that reality is brutal, that 'Facts *are* nasty' (Ch. 3). These realists substitute for 'heart' something that Herzog calls 'potato love', a meaningless, sentimental pretence of emotion.

Herzog's own main engagement with modern love comes, of course, in his relationships with women. He is trying to detach himself emotionally from his ex-wife Madeleine who is, at least as perceived by Herzog, a misogynist's vision of female beauty, a devouring demon-woman (perhaps here Bellow is taking a little personal revenge). Completely uprooting him by taking control of his life after their marriage, the emotionally unbalanced Madeleine suddenly decided she no longer wished to be married to him, and this is the source of his current perturbation. He sees himself as a victim, and blames Madeleine for her failure properly to value him, but in fact he has had problems with all his women. His first wife Daisy was the opposite of Madeleine, a model of order and stability, but that marriage failed. Ramona, his current mistress, is beautiful, loving, sexy, intelligent, almost a wish-fulfilment figure, but she wants to possess him, and he half wishes to escape from her. His wistful memories of the Japanese child-woman Sono perhaps indicate that the problem lies with Herzog himself, that there is something undeveloped in him that wants to evade the responsibilities of an adult relationship.

Herzog's sense of being victimized by Madeleine grows into a more general sense of injury, and this becomes inextricable from his view of himself as the representative of values that are under pressure. The comedy of the novel develops out of the gap between his intellectual finesse and his hapless blundering in the world. It is a gap that is eventually illuminated for Herzog by his past friend and current rival Valentine Gersbach. Gersbach is a device brilliantly used here by Bellow, a parodic alter ego; Herzog thinks: 'People say that Gersbach imitates me – my walk, my expressions. He's a second Herzog' (Ch. 5). This debased version of teacher-Herzog is a pop-intellectual in love with his own ideas; he hires a hall in which to read his own poetry and weeps before a vast audience; he misuses ideas as he misuses Yiddish phrases. Like Herzog he is a sufferer, 'a frequent weeper of distinguished emotional power' (Ch. 2). His suffering, like everything else about him, is described in hyperbole, exaggerated to a degree where it becomes little more than a histrionic gesture, collapsing into absurdity. This is true of his ideas, too; Herzog remembers him reading lectures that 'were so spirited, so vehement, gross, they were ludicrous too, a parody of the intellectual's desire for higher meaning, depth, quality' (Ch. 2). Here is an ironic commentary on Herzog's own intellectual productions, providing one way, at least, of reading his letters.

This pseudo-Herzog Gersbach has a further function, for he reveals Herzog's own projected guilt. Herzog has failed as father and husband, and Gersbach has assumed his position as both. It is here where Herzog finds his chief cause for resentment: 'if he took away my wife, did he have to suffer my agony for me too? Because he could do even that better?' (Ch. 6). The bitter irony in Herzog's words here is not directed at Gersbach's performance, but at his own failure. Because he has retired into a world of ideas he has evaded reality: 'Moses refused to know evil. But he could not refuse to experience it. And therefore others were appointed to do it to him, and then to be accused (by him) of wickedness' (Ch. 7). It is this structural relationship with Gersbach that leads Herzog to a kind of epiphany, a moment of sudden revelation about the true nature of his state that is part of his recuperation. It occurs when he goes to Madeleine's house in Chicago with the intention of killing her and Gersbach. Looking through the bathroom window he sees the daughter he loves being tenderly bathed by Gersbach, and is suddenly unable to act: 'As soon as Herzog saw the actual person giving an actual bath, the reality of it, the tenderness of such a buffoon to a little child, his intended violence turned into *theatre*, into something ludicrous'. He discovers the inauthénticity, the melodrama of his attitude, as he becomes aware of Gersbach as a scapegoat, a stand-in whom he has employed to allow him to conceal from himself the real cause of his problems: 'Only self-hatred could lead him to ruin himself because his heart was "broken". How could it be broken by such a pair?' (Ch. 7).

This discovery is one of the things that lead Herzog to the serenity of his New England garden and the silence of the novel's ending. But it is part of a process that actually takes place in the garden, since the whole narrative is Herzog's meditation there, his reconstruction of fragmented experience to find a new sense of coherence that will allow a reassertion of identity. At the centre of his meditation is the memory of his Montreal childhood, of the love and connectedness it represents. Memory can be cruel in what it selects, as Herzog notes of his own: 'all the dead and the mad are in my custody, and I am the nemesis of the would-be forgotten. I bind others to my feelings and oppress them' (Ch. 4). But like other later Bellow heroes, Herzog discovers that memory can be a source of consolation and emotional nourishment (once again the Words-worth of such poems of memory and childhood as the 'Immortal-ity Ode' and 'Tintern Abbey' is influential). Paradise is lost, but something of what it means can be regained through recollection, and this is what allows Herzog his moment of equilibrium in his garden, temporary though it may be. It is no accident that his presence there is due to his brother Will, and that he is spending his time painting a piano for his daughter. These old sources of love, newly tapped, make him weep and provide him with some relief: 'It's only love. Or something that bears down like love. It probably is love' (Ch. 9).

Bellow saw *Herzog* as the end of a literary development, but looking back it can be seen equally as the start of another one. The device of Herzog's letters allowed Bellow to import into his novel a huge amount of intellectual material. Herzog's mind ranges over the ideas that have produced the modern world, but it does so in the vernacular rhythms of the earlier novels, emerging as a voice that is distinctively 'Bellovian'. The problem here is that the ideas sometimes get in the way of the story-telling. Bellow's attempt to equate Herzog's spiritual state as induced by his personal emotion-al experiences with the spiritual state of representative modern man doesn't always come off. We cannot easily see how Herzog's optimistic rejection of the negative modernist 'wasteland' mentality, 'the cheap mental stimulants of Alienation' (Ch. 3), relates to his victory over the self-pity generated by his treatment by Madeleine. But as the comedy of a man swamped by ideas, struggling to find those that he can live by, *Herzog* works very well.

One of the critical problems with *Herzog* is that what we know of the protagonist's experience hardly convinces us that he seriously suffers, while his own obsession with his 'suffering' inclines him constantly towards self-pity. The protagonist of Bellow's next novel, *Mr. Sammler's Planet* (1969), has genuinely suffered, but he demonstrates no self-pity. Rather, he is concerned to analyse the meaning of his experience and to relate it to his 'planet', the America of the late sixties that he sees about him, of which he is a harsh judge. As was the case with *Herzog*, the novel is essentially about its protagonist's consciousness, and takes its form from what he perceives. Mr Artur Sammler is a man in his seventies, a Polish Jew who came to America after World War II. His early history is only vaguely represented: he was brought up in an apparently wealthy and certainly intellectually cultivated household, and lived in London for some years before the war, serving as a correspondent for certain Polish journals. In London he developed connections with the Bloomsbury Group and became an associate of H. G. Wells, and this English influence affected him profoundly. He was, however, affected much more profoundly by his wartime experience in Poland, where he had gone immediately prior to the war. Arrested by the Nazis, he and his wife were forced, along with many other Jews, to dig a mass grave for themselves, and were then shot. Mr Sammler alone survived, struggling through a heap of bodies to climb from the grave; his sightless eye is a souvenir of this experience. Driven to hide in the Zamosht Forest he joined the Polish partisans (it was during this time that he killed a German prisoner) but at the end of the war the Poles too turned on the Jews, and Sammler once again survived a massacre and once again experienced the grave, hiding for a summer in a mausoleum. These Holocaust images haunt Mr Sammler and haunt the novel (his sensations as he struggles through the pressure of bodies in a crowded bus and his fear of going underground to take the train are revivals of memories of the grave). After the war Mr Sammler and his daughter Shula were brought from a displaced persons' camp to New York by Sammler's nephew Elya Gruner and have lived, up to the time of the events of the novel, on Gruner's charity.

The actual events recounted in the novel take place over a period of about three days during which Mr Sammler is concerned about Elya Gruner's impending death, for Gruner is the person Sammler values most in the world, and Sammler wants to think of some word of consolation that he can take to the dying man. But he comes into contact with a variety of more-or-less mad individuals who provide him with a number of distracting experiences. He gives a disastrous talk at Columbia University because he is misled by his student contact, Lionel Feffer ('less student than promoter'), about the expectations of his audience; he observes a black pickpocket at work and finds himself menaced by him; he has to listen unwillingly to Gruner's children, to the sexual problems of his daughter Angela and to the money-making schemes of his son Wallace, and to put up with the artistic pretensions of his own son-in-law Eisen. Most distressing to him is the theft by his daughter Shula of a manuscript belonging to an Indian professor, Dr Govinda Lal. Sammler's attempt to recover the manuscript and return it to Lal leads to a near-farcical journey round New York and a meeting with the professor which develops into a very lengthy dialogue about the future of mankind. When finally he is on his way to the dying Elya he intervenes in a confrontation between Feffer and the black pickpocket and, by involving Eisen, becomes responsible for an act of horrifying violence. With all this he fails to reach Elya in time, and is left to say a prayer over his dead nephew's body.

Although *Mr. Sammler's Planet* contains much of the kind of comedy that is characteristic of Bellow, its overall tone is undeniably sombre, and the methods of its composition and the unusual circumstances of its publication show how much care Bellow took to achieve this tone. *Mr. Sammler's Planet* was published in two versions. It made its first appearance as a two-part serial in the November and December 1969 issues of the *Atlantic Monthly* magazine, and was put out in book form in the following year by the Viking Press. The fact that there are numerous differences between the two versions shows how rigorous and painstaking Bellow is in his writing: even in the later stages of production of the novel he was still making alterations, still trying to refine it. Indeed, the various surviving manuscripts that relate to *Mr. Sammler's Planet* provide an excellent demonstration of how he goes about the process of writing. The Department of Special Collections at the library of the University of Chicago contains, amongst other *Sammler* materials, some pages of a manuscript deposited there in 1967 that are clearly the seed of the novel, even though their protagonist is named Meyer Pawlyk and their setting is Chicago. There is also a finished version, written in manuscript in four notebooks, entitled *The Future of the Moon*. Two typescripts, carbon and xerox copies of them, and the proofs of both the *Atlantic* and the Viking versions, all contain extensive annotations and revisions, indicating that for Bellow the process of composition ends only when it has to, with publication.[51] One notable difference between the two publications is that the *Atlantic Monthly* version is accompanied by black and white drawings of depressed urban scenes that draw attention to the gloomier aspects of the novel.

The urban landscape of *Mr. Sammler's Planet* is, no doubt, a depressing one, and one with which the protagonist is totally out of sympathy. The individuals who populate it are also rather disturbing: grotesque, often comically so, but also repellent because they are arrested in a state of childish self-absorption. This 'planet' is subjected to analysis through the vast intellectual paraphernalia of Mr Sammler's reading (which is also, of course, Bellow's reading) and through his personal experience, so that the novel is also built out of the materials of his cultural and personal history. The contemporary world is generally an object of Mr Sammler's contempt, and since it is seen only from his perspective, the novel apparently invites us to share his judgement. Consequently, like *Herzog*, he has often been seen as a mouthpiece for Bellow's own judgements. Alfred Kazin, in his review of the novel thought Mr Sammler to be 'so openly Bellow's mind now, in its most minute qualifications', and he found the identification disturbing: 'Sammler's opinions are set in a context so uncharitable, morally arrogant toward every other character in the book but one, and therefore lacking in dramatic satisfaction, that the book becomes a *cri du coeur* that does not disguise the punitive moral outrage behind it'.[52]

It cannot be denied that the book seems to invite this identification. The incident in Chapter 1, for example, in which Mr Sammler gives a seminar at Columbia University to an audience that is both youthful and uncomprehending, and is humiliated when a vast and unexpected chasm opens between him and his hearers, clearly had its genesis in a very similar experience that Bellow had when he gave a talk at San Francisco State College.[53] The novel is obsessed by the implications of this chasm, by what it sees as the total dislocation of the younger generation from the values of the past. To put this obsession into perspective a brief consideration of the political climate at the end of the sixties is necessary.

The early years of the decade were marked by an optimism that developed around the confidence and charisma of John F. Kennedy and the group of youthful and energetic intellectuals who advised him. Americans believed the country was about to move into a period of progress and achievement driven by the pragmatic liberalism of the Kennedy party that would open up what was referred to as the 'New Frontier'. By the end of the sixties the dream of the New Frontier was in ruins, the euphoria replaced by a sense of frustration and defeat. The causes of this change are very complex, but they can be located around two major issues of moral concern. First, America's racial problems took on a public prominence that they had never had before. The growing pressure of the civil rights movement in the Southern states led to a new concern with ideas of freedom and political morality. The horrendous repression of blacks that marked the Southern resistance to desegregation culminated, in the spring of 1965, in the violent confrontations that took place in Selma, Alabama, which were followed by widespread racial unrest, especially in Northern cities, resulting in the appearance of the Black Panthers and the growth of the Black Power movement. The other major issue that led to massive protest was the on-going agony of the war in Vietnam. In 1965 a group that called itself Students for a Democratic Society organized a march on Washington to protest against the war, initiating a series of student demonstrations that continued into the seventies.

These two great sources of social conflict coincided with the emergence of what can only be called a 'youth culture'. The children born in the post-war baby-boom and brought up in an affluence and with an indulgence that their parents had not experienced were coming of age in the late sixties. They were confronted with the two moral-political issues of racism at home and a bloody war abroad in which those in authority, who represented their parents' generation, seemed to be acting with cruel intransigence, and their response was a general rejection of established values. Many slogans were coined to define this rejection: 'counterculture', 'drop out', 'flower-power'; the emphasis was on spiritual self-development rather than sterile materialism, and on an individual freedom that expressed itself particularly through sexual liberation and was therefore an attack on traditional values and, especially, on the family. This is the point at which Bellow's Mr Sammler stands, observing a world of young people who have cut themselves off from history by denying the values that history has brought to them. Sammler is a commentator, and a very partial one, on the 'generation gap'. But in spite of the tone of much of what he thinks and says about the deficiencies of young people it will not do to see him simply as a querulous old man envious of youthful energies, the spokesman for a novelist who can see nothing in the world to like. For Bellow has more serious fears about the dangers that open up before those who refuse to learn the lessons of history, fears that originate in the nightmare of the Holocaust. Although some of his earlier novels, most notably *The Victim,* concern Jewish experience of anti-Semitism, this is the first to have the Nazi pogroms as one of its central preoccupations.

In 1967 Bellow went to Sinai to report for *Newsday* magazine on the Six-Day War, and much of what he saw there emerges as part of Mr Sammler's experience. Unlike six million other Jews, Sammler himself had survived the Holocaust, literally rising from the grave. The threat of the Arab countries allied against Israel raised the possibility of a repetition of the Holocaust, as Sammler plainly sees: 'for the second time in twenty-five years the same people were threatened by extermination: the so-called powers letting things drift toward disaster; men armed for a massacre' (Ch. 3). As it turned out there was no new Holocaust, and indeed the Israelis themselves emerged triumphant from this war, but the possibility of a repetition of history was there. These issues form a complex part of the novel's concerns. Mr Sammler is haunted by his memory of the moment when he killed the German prisoner in the Zamosht Forest. He acknowledges that this act was murder, but he believes that his own experience of extreme suffering at the hands of the Germans made his act inevitable. What disturbs him about the event, however, is that he felt an undeniable joy in his act of power, and this has taught him that the potential for violence and joy in violence is in all men. In the same way, the Israelis were compromised in the Sinai War when they used napalm while denying they were using it – a violence gone beyond the needs of the situation. This is what makes the act of violence committed by Eisen against the black thief so horrifying to Mr Sammler: Eisen equates his own violence with Sammler's, with nothing of the sense

of the moral impropriety of the act that Sammler has. It is the lack
of this ability to make distinctions that Sammler sees everywhere
about him.

The importance of the figure of Mr Sammler lies in his relation
to history. He is, as he himself sees, a symbol: 'Mr Sammler had a
symbolic character. He, personally, was a symbol. His friends and
family had made him a judge and a priest. And of what was he a
symbol? He didn't even know. Was it because he had survived?'
(Ch. 2). Survival is certainly a part of it, but what is it that has
survived? Sammler embodies the humane thought of his own past
and his own vast reading, 'foreign, Polish Oxonian', the Old World
culture of Europe modified by the optimistic thought of H. G.
Wells and the Bloomsbury Group, the conviction that human
affairs can be conducted with intelligence and compassion. But he
also embodies the extremity of suffering, having experienced
totalitarian aggression almost to the point of annihilation. As
Gerald Graff puts it, 'Sammler's past makes him a nexus of the
historical forces, both hopeful and destructive, whose collision has
created the present-day world'.[54] But he has survived into a world
in which all the liberal values of the past that he carries with him
have been distorted into modes of personal freedom that are a
self-indulgent mockery of true civilization.

The vast weight of this historical culture makes for an artistically
uncomfortable form, since much of the text consists of a bald
presentation of Mr Sammler's (Bellow's?) ideas about the state of
things, and *Mr. Sammler's Planet* has been criticized for its failure to
integrate its intellectual content into its imaginative vision (the
Sammler-Lal dialogue in Chapter 5 is the example usually given to
support this criticism). The polemic, in this view, gets in the way of
the story. Nevertheless, Sammler is an extraordinary construction,
a fusion of an immense range of Western thought and writing with
the fundamental formative experiences of the twentieth century.
Although he is a harsh judge of the society in which he moves his
main concern is with the location of something that can be valued.
He moves, however, in a world in which people value only what is
fatuous.

If we take the two major criticisms of the novel – that it is an arid
presentation of Bellow's own embittered vision of the modern
world, and that its artistic form collapses under its intellectual
weight – we may consider that they arise from a misunderstanding
of what Bellow is trying to do. The novel itself insists on the

limitations of all perspectives: Mr Sammler's good eye observes the external world, but his other eye, destroyed at the moment of his confrontation with death, is the inward eye that looks on more urgent matters but can distinguish only light and shade. Sammler himself 'felt that the way he saw things could not be right. His experiences had been too peculiar, and he feared that he projected peculiarities onto life. Life was probably not blameless, but he often thought that life was not and could not be what he was seeing' (Ch. 3). We are not being told explicitly that the perspective of the novel is distorted, but we are being warned about the possibility. There is, too, the novel's insistent move towards the comic that brings in a degree of scepticism towards Sammler's pretensions. For example, the lengthy dialogue with Lal that so many readers have found tedious is deflated when it is literally washed out by Wallace Gruner's flood.

Still, the planet seen here *is* Mr Sammler's, and we must look at what he sees. The New York of the novel is the ruined urban landscape by now familiar in Bellow's work. But, as Sammler sees it, it is the location of a new barbarism that has erupted because values are now dictated by the young, by what Sammler calls the 'sovereign youth-style' (Ch. 1). He sees a new generation, a 'crazy species', who have rejected the values of their parents and asserted their own independence (like Wallace Gruner who expresses contempt for the ways in which his father made his money but is anxious to get his own hands on it so that he can live freely in his own way). This independence, however, has led to an obsession with originality that is in fact the emulation of false models emptied of significance, the 'imitative anarchy of the streets' (Ch. 3) – revolution as fashion. Seeking their own reality and denying all the old standards, the young, Sammler thinks, have found only excrement and aggression to put in their place, 'All this confused sex-excrement-militancy, explosiveness, abusiveness, tooth-showing, Barbary ape howling' (Ch. 1). Like the Yahoos in *Gulliver's Travels* they seem to embrace all that is not civilized.

It is the 'sex-excrement-militancy' conjunction that is the problem. A key scene in the early part of the novel is that in which Sammler attempts to give a seminar on the Bloomsbury group to an audience of students who are expecting to hear about Sorel and modern violence. Georges Sorel, who wrote *Reflections on Violence* (1915), was an admirer of Nietzsche, and believed that violence was the only possible path of salvation for the modern world. No one who wants to hear about this could be expected to be interested in Sammler's reminiscences about a group of benevolent, Utopian intellectuals. What horrifies him is not so much his audience's lack of interest in what he has to say as the hostility against him personally for saying it. The seminar is broken up by a young man, a 'figure of compact distortion', who asks the audience: ' "Why do you listen to this effete old shit? What has he got to tell you? His balls are dry. He's dead. He can't come." ' (Ch. 1). The distinction between generations is rendered to a simple matter of sexual potency. The old are impotent and therefore they are dead and can have nothing to say. Potency is turned into a weapon, but sex itself, in Mr Sammler's view, is rendered sterile, turned into excrement, when used in this way.

Or when used in any 'modern' way. In someone like Feffer, a seducer and user of men's wives, sex is sterile because it is just another of the means by which he controls and manipulates the world about him. More insidious is the debased romantic idea that freedom means sexual freedom, and Angela Gruner, the character who most opulently represents this view, has also rendered sex sterile. Angela is the novel's embodiment of misdirected erotic energy. Her sexuality is described as an overpowering animal force: 'Cheeks bursting with color, eyes dark sexual blue, a white vital heat in the flesh of the throat, she carried a great statement to males, the powerful message of gender' (Ch. 2). She is a sexual explorer, acting out an ideological theory of sexual liberation, apparently willing to try anything with anybody. At the same time she craves love and cannot understand that such sexual liberation is not compatible with love. She cannot understand why, after a mate-swapping session in Acapulco, her lover Wharton Horricker should be reluctant to marry her; while seeing nothing perverse in her actions she ironically sees Horricker's jealousy as perverse.

This sexual anarchy is only a part of what has happened in a world in which, it seems to Sammler, the children have released themselves from all moral and intellectual control into madness. The word '*Sammler*' in German means 'collector', and Mr Sammler thinks of himself as a collector of crazy people, 'confidant of New York eccentrics; curate of wild men and progenitor of a wild woman; registrar of madness' (Ch. 3). He has collected a series of self-absorbed people, all somehow unable to move out of a childish state. Wallace Gruner is 'genuinely loony', a brilliant young man who cannot carry through any of the eccentric projects he initiates.

Sammler's own daughter Shula is also mad, a 'nut', a bewigged bag-lady who has lost any moral sense except insofar as it concerns the well-being of her father. Her husband Eisen is a 'cheerful maniac', an artist who has somehow created an art that turns its subjects into corpses, and who turns his own art-objects literally into a lethal weapon. Angela's sexuality is really a cult of the body, and her lover Horricker takes the same narcissism to an extreme, obsessed with his own body as a work of art to be elegantly clothed.

These characters share an eccentric energy that gives them an almost Dickensian grotesqueness, and we laugh at them. But there is also something in them that disturbs us and that goes beyond laughter, and it can best be seen in the figure of Walter Bruch. Bruch, in his sixties, is a musicologist, a man committed to one form of history, the discovery and performance of ancient music. But Bruch has a curious sexual perversion that impels him to masturbate at the sight of women's arms. This is, in fact, an addiction from which Bruch wishes to free himself but cannot. To console himself he buys toys and plays with them alone in his room. This is a chilling image of a man who is a prey to sterile sexual impulses, frozen in a childish state, and it is an image that casts its shadow on the other 'children' of the novel.

What is to be set up against all this chaos on Mr Sammler's planet? Can an answer be found in Sammler's own intellectual training, in all those Utopians, philosophers and theorists who fill his thoughts? Sammler, we are told, was christened Artur after the philosopher Artur Schopenhauer, who was himself a pessimist. Schopenhauer's principle work is *The World as Will and Idea* (1818), in which he theorized about a wicked cosmic will that ensures endless suffering in life and a futile struggle against an inevitable death. H. G. Wells, on the other hand, who is central to much of what Sammler thinks, was an optimist, believing that human life could be improved by the application of rational scientific principles. But having read widely in writers who have tried to explain the world Sammler has become convinced that neither Utopianists nor those who believe in power have the answers, and now finds his consolation mainly in the writings of the medieval mystic Meister Eckhart, who counselled that God's comfort can be found only by turning away from this world.

And yet this is something that Mr Sammler cannot do. The Apollo moonshot, which is taking place in the background of the novel, is an appropriate metaphor for turning away from this world, and in his long dialogue with Dr Lal Sammler considers the significance of the moon. Lal has an eschatological vision of the future of this crowded planet, believing that a final explosion is imminent. But also, somewhat like Wells, he thinks that an escape from this world will be possible, a jumping off to the moon, through the application of technology. Mr Sammler resists this; he believes that the problems of this world must be faced here on this planet. Dr Lal is one of the few people in the novel that Sammler finds himself able to approve of, but in a sense he is deluded by his own ideas, and the moon represents this delusion.

The image of the moon functions in the novel in a highly complex manner. The moon has a long history as a symbol of the ideal: pure, white, distant, an unattainable object of desire; most notable in this respect is its classical association with chastity, and considering the novel's preoccupation with sexual liberation, the frequent reference to the moon provides a wry comment on modern practices. But Mr Sammler's moon is about to be drained of its mystical meanings, for the implication of the Apollo moon-shot is that this impossibly remote object will soon be attained, will become, indeed, of no more significance than any other tourist attraction that people like Wallace Gruner can visit on charter flights. So while the possibilities of positive illusion that the moon once offered are lost, its connections with more sinister delusions remain: madness, monomania, moon-driven obsession. Lunacy is, at least according to Mr Sammler, the perennial state of most of the characters in the novel.

Perhaps all men need what the moon offers, however, whether it be illusion or delusion, ideal or mania, for Sammler has his own moon in the figure of Elya Gruner. During his conversation with Dr Lal, Sammler cannot get the image of his nephew out of his mind: 'Elya reappeared strangely and continually, as if his face were orbiting – as if he were a satellite' (Ch. 5). Elya is the moral centre of the novel; on him Sammler projects his own need for a corrective to the idiocies of the world. He is a man, as Sammler says in the closing passage of the novel, who has done 'what was required of him', who has met 'the terms of his contract'. Under-standing the need for commitment, he persevered in his profession of gynaecology, even though he disliked it. Like Sammler, he is aware of the importance of maintaining contact with history. Impelled by 'Old World family feelings' (Ch. 1) he rescued Sam-mler and his daughter from the DP camp in 1947, and has maintained them ever since. His favourite pastime is the construction of genealogies, the objective proof of his connectedness with the past: 'He had a passion for kinships' (Ch. 2). Like Sammler, he values the Old World virtues of courtesy and generosity, virtues that recognize the worth of other people and the importance of connectedness, of what in other words might be called love. Kinship, commitment, a sense of the importance of the past: these are the things that Sammler seeks to set in opposition to the fatuousness of the young, who lack both courtesy and dignity. He is proud of his own manners, and he sees a reflection of them in Elya's faithful old driver Emil (who is associated with the 'dignified' Rolls Royce) and in Dr Lal (who is a 'gentleman'). This is what marks, for Sammler, the crucial difference between Elya Gruner and the generation of madmen who, like the heckler at the Columbia lecture, know nothing of courtesy. Between Sammler and Elya there is a bond of mutual need, and it is Sammler's growing sense of loss that provides the novel with its emotional weight.

This denial of the modern world in favour of old-fashioned 'manners' might seem sentimental if it were not for the fact that it emerges from Mr Sammler's own deeply-felt experience. We are not, however, being offered this as a final judgement on the world. At one point Mr Sammler remembers the old saying that provided the seed for a story by Wells that 'in the country of the blind the one-eyed man is king'. Perhaps what is demonstrated in one-eyed Mr Sammler is that even the wisest of men are only partially-sighted, for he has his own blind spots. He ignores, for example, the implications of the possibility that Elya, a man whose profession was to give life, had performed abortions for the wealthy and well-connected. He also fails to note Gruner's spectacular parental failure to communicate his own values to his children. Further, Sammler's general contempt for women makes it impossible for him to take seriously even the generous Margotte, who is 'boundlessly, achingly, hopelessly on the right side, the best side, of every big human question' (Ch. 1). Perhaps the most puzzling example of his faulty vision is his sympathetic reaction to the black pickpocket. He sees the man as an outsider like himself, and admires his animal power and arrogance. It is particularly difficult to explain his own lack of compassion for the weak old man who is victimized by the black, for this is a kind of terrorism hardly different from what Sammler experienced at the hands of the Nazis. In addition, when

the black exhibits his penis to Mr Sammler he is equating his own
superior power with sexual potency, an equation that Sammler so
strongly resents when it is made by the young man at his lecture.

It is in such ambiguities as these that we see the distance between
Mr Sammler and Bellow. Though much of what Sammler thinks
about the modern world is what Bellow thinks, he is not Bellow's
mouthpiece. He is an independent creation, a serious figure whose
experiences and sensibility give him the authority to judge the
world, while also disabling him from a totally impartial judgement.
And when he takes himself too seriously, he is liable to be comically
undercut, his ideas washed away in a lunatic flood, or his shoes
baked by his mad daughter. His affirmation at the end of the novel
as he prays over Gruner's body may seem an optimistic conclusion
to a pessimistic novel and, like the affirmative endings of earlier
novels, has been criticized, but Mr Sammler is a man who has
earned his right to an affirmation, a man who has proved himself
as a survivor by struggling out of the grave, a man who, despite his
recognition that life is a place of degraded clowning, is doing his
best, trying to find the good, trying to fulfil the terms of his
contract.

By the late sixties Bellow's popular success had brought him a
substantial income, along with the problems that go with such
wealth. His success also made him into a public figure, someone
who appeared to have the ear of the nation, someone whose ideas
were actually heard (though as Sammler's depressing experience
with his lecture to the Columbia students suggests, being heard is
not the same thing as being listened to). It is not surprising that he
should have become concerned about the effects of such success on
his obligations to his art, and in Charlie Citrine, the protagonist of
Humboldt's Gift, he presents the first of his heroes actually to be a
literary 'artist'. Citrine ponders just the kind of question that must
have been exercising Bellow at the time: What happens to the
writer who, seeking truth and beauty, somehow finds 'the big
money' also? As Citrine says, 'such sums as I made, made themselves. Capitalism made them for dark comical reasons of its own'
(Ch. 1). The material rewards are not conferred upon the writer
for what he has achieved, because capitalism does not understand
that achievement. Consequently, the writer himself may be misled
by his apparent triumph, and may be corrupted into equating his
material rewards with artistic success: 'To make capitalists out of
artists was a humorous idea of some depth. America decided to test

the pretensions of the aesthetic by applying the dollar measure'
(Ch.31). Bellow saw clearly that what he as a writer was trying to
communicate and what his public understood were not necessarily
the same thing, that there was a disjunction between the writer and
the public figure of the writer: 'the success meant that I was
supplying a need, a public need – of a cultural kind. And that I was
expected to act the cultural figure, to be a public utility, an unpaid
functionary, something between a congressman and a
clergyman'.[55] Bellow clearly had these issues very much in mind as
he was writing *Humboldt's Gift*.

Humboldt's Gift was published in 1975. More than eight years
went into its composition (early manuscripts related to the novel
date from before *Mr. Sammler's Planet*), and it is in many ways
Bellow's richest and most complex work. It is built out of a wide
range of themes and preoccupations, and functions on many levels,
but amongst its central concerns is the status of the artist in the
modern technocratic-business world. This question is explored
through a number of interconnected issues: the agony of the
individual poet in a mass society, the relationship between art and
business, the relationship between the spiritual and the material,
the dislocation of modern American culture from its European
history, the importance of memory, the meaning of love, the future
of the soul. This list by no means exhausts the sweep of the novel's
interests. Although its preoccupations are serious, even potentially
tragic, the vision of *Humboldt's Gift* is blackly comic. Its protagonist,
Charlie Citrine, becomes the hapless victim of a series of often-
farcical events that strip him of his money and his dignity, as he
moves through a world populated by characters who are grotesque
in their predatory voraciousness but who are endowed with a
manic comic energy.

Humboldt's Gift began as a memoir of Bellow's friend Delmore
Schwartz. Schwartz was a gifted poet and short-story writer whom
Bellow had met at Princeton. His volume of stories and poems, *In
Dreams Begin Responsibilities* (1938), had made him a leading figure
in the group of New York Jewish writers and intellectuals that
emerged in the thirties and forties, but he was unable to deal with
his success. He suffered from paranoia and manic-depression, and,
like Humboldt, became addicted to pills and alcohol, eventually
declining into dereliction and, in 1966, dying of a heart attack.
Bellow had seen him on the streets some weeks before his death
and had been unable to face him; the memoir was a kind of

penance.[56] It is easy to see how the figure of Humboldt developed from this memoir, though, of course, the fictional figure is no longer precisely Schwartz, whose literary career, despite its decline, was somewhat more substantial than Humboldt's. The dangerous dynamics of the relationship between the writer and his audience were obviously something that Bellow felt merited investigation, however, and this he did through two figures: Von Humboldt Fleisher, and his friend and disciple, the narrator of Humboldt's story, Charlie Citrine.

In spite of what we might expect from the novel's title and from its genesis in the Schwartz memoir, Humboldt is not quite at its centre, for his importance lies in the way in which his life is understood and reconstructed by Citrine. Citrine is a figure much more like Bellow himself, and the novel contains many autobiographical elements apart from the relationship with Humboldt: Citrine's intellectual interests, his awards and prizes, including the Croix de Chevalier des Arts et Lettres, his problems with wives and lawyers, his public reputation. As with earlier novels, the narrative voice is enclosed within the protagonist's perspective, encouraging us to think of Citrine's voice as if it were Bellow's. But while acknowledging the increasing difficulty in these later novels of separating Bellow from his protagonists, we must guard against the temptation to identify him too closely with them.

Charlie Citrine is a successful writer in his mid-fifties, author of a Broadway hit called *Von Trenck*, and Pulitzer Prize-winning historian and biographer. He has all the rewards of success: fame, an expensive life-style and, most important, a beautiful mistress named Renata Koffritz. He is also, however, suffering the consequences of success. An alimony battle with his ex-wife Denise means that his money is being drained away by lawyers and judges. He is involved in a literary venture with his charming but irresponsible friend Pierre Thaxter to set up a journal called *The Ark*, and this too is losing money for him. He owes money to the taxman and to publishers who have given him advances for books he will never write. And Renata is putting pressure on him to marry her. Further, he is intensely aware of approaching old age, to which he responds with an undignified attempt to cling to youth, and a growing preoccupation with death and the frustrating question of immortality.

The novel is, in effect, Citrine's monologue. Like *Herzog*, it is presented not in chapters, but as a series of unnumbered sections that allow Bellow great flexibility in leading Citrine through meditations on his past, on world history, on his present experiences, and on immortality. This method allows the juxtaposition of a range of styles, from the racy vernacular of the Chicago streets to the often abstract language of Citrine's metaphysical broodings. Its effect is the parallel presentation of the outer and inner or material and spiritual worlds as Citrine perceives them. Underlying this rather loose narrative structure is another structure, a cyclical one that presents the experience of the writer in modern society through the inter-connected careers of Humboldt and Citrine. Humboldt's career began with the brilliant success in the thirties of his volume of poems *Harlequin Ballads*, but declined in the forties and fifties into failure, violence and madness, ending with his squalid death in the mid-sixties. Citrine's life as a writer began with his eager introduction to the bohemian life as Humboldt's disciple, but went in a different direction with the popular success in the early fifties of *Von Trenck*; his success has continued right up to the time that constitutes the 'present' of the novel, the five months from December 1973 to April 1974.

During those five months Citrine goes through a series of experiences that show him the world from a new perspective and radically change his view of himself and of his success. A small-time gangster called Rinaldo Cantabile involves him in a series of comically threatening or humiliating incidents that introduce him to certain Chicago realities. Concurrently, he is introduced to another kind of reality by the courts when it is made clear to him that he will never be able to settle enough on Denise to satisfy her, and that the law has no sympathy for him. To get away from these pressures he flees to Europe, where he expects to be with Renata, but instead finds himself in Madrid looking after her mother and young son. Belatedly deciding that it is the only way to secure Renata he proposes to her, only to learn that it is too late because she has married an affluent undertaker called Flonzaley. Alone in Madrid, and near to destitution, he finally receives Humboldt's gift.

The nature of the gift referred to in the novel's title is fundamental to its meaning. At the literal level the gift is the legacy that Humboldt wills to Citrine, the filmscript that repairs the latter's fortunes. But the word 'gift' refers also to Humboldt's poetic genius, the ability that held so much promise and that was blocked and squandered in self-destructive paranoia. As viewed by

Citrine, Humboldt was the embodiment of the romantic idea of the poet, a kind of incarnation of the image that appears at the end of Coleridge's poem 'Kubla Khan':

> Beware! Beware!
> His flashing eyes, his floating hair!
> Weave a circle round him thrice,
> And close your eyes with holy dread,
> For he on honey-dew hath fed,
> And drunk the milk of Paradise.

This image of the poet, separated by his vision from the normal, 'real' world, is important to Citrine who, in spite of his early adulation of this visionary Humboldt and his desire to think of himself as an artist, is, in fact, a writer of a different kind. Citrine has made a fortune from his profession, won the prizes that demonstrate establishment recognition, and become a celebrity, on nodding terms with the rich and powerful – as a writer he is quite acceptable in the real world.

In spite of Citrine's desire to idealize Humboldt, it is fairly apparent that the poet had ordinary, materialist impulses. The year 1953 had been a turning point for the two men. Humboldt had hoped that the liberal intellectual Adlai Stevenson would win the presidential election and would promote men like him, but the defeat of Stevenson by Eisenhower crushed Humboldt's hopes and destroyed his chance of getting an endowed chair at Princeton. In the same year Citrine's play *Von Trench* became a hit, upsetting envious Humboldt, who turned mockingly hostile to Citrine. The two men were estranged, and Citrine did not see Humboldt again for fifteen years; in New York City he unexpectedly came upon the now down-and-out poet and hid because he was unable to bring himself to talk to him. Humboldt died shortly after, and now, some six or seven years on, Citrine is haunted by a sense of guilt at this betrayal of his friend. Humboldt has become a part of his inner world, for Citrine uses him as a subject of meditation. This is Humboldt's real gift to his disciple: in his attempts to understand the meaning of Humboldt's failed life Citrine begins to see the meaning of his own 'successful' career. He meditates on the past, and especially on the figure of the dead poet, taking in questions about the value of poetry, the place of intellectual endeavour in a money-driven culture, the possibility of personal relationships, the restorative function of memory, and what he calls 'the death question'.

Like Herzog, Citrine spends much of his novel reclining in the familiar meditative position of Wordsworth in 'Tintern Abbey' working over the past in an attempt at 'tranquil restoration'. The idea of the writer embraced both by Humboldt and by Citrine is essentially a romantic one: the poet is dedicated to the pursuit of beauty and spiritual ideals, to some sort of higher truth, which he has to communicate to the world at large. He is the Orphic leader who can actually make things happen with his art, becoming the 'radiant centre of his age' (Ch. 2). Humboldt, at least as Citrine constructs him in memory, was such a figure. We can see from his conversations, as recorded by Citrine, that he was a charismatic, exciting talker, ranging widely through his reading and playing with exhilarating, risky ideas, and we can see him as a man who might be destroyed by the demands of his creative energies. But we are constrained by the narrative perspective to see Humboldt as Citrine chooses to see him, and we should note the things that Citrine glosses over: Humboldt's deviousness, his envious spite, the irrational violence that drove his wife away. And, in spite of Citrine's attempt to fit him into the figure of the archetypal poet, we should recognize that Humboldt wanted the rewards of popular success.

Why does Citrine need to idealize Humboldt? The cycles of the literary careers of the two men seem to show contrasting patterns of failure and success, but Citrine, in his account of Humboldt, attributes the poet's failure to his refusal to compromise his values in the face of the philistine indifference of the public, thus turning the failure into a kind of moral victory. If Humboldt can be seen as a success in this way, then in the same terms Citrine himself has failed, because his success has arisen precisely from his ability to please that same philistine audience. Although he wishes to see himself as a true artist his play *Von Trench* seems, from what we are told of it, to be something of a lowbrow pot-boiler, and his subsequent fame has come from his marginally literary work in journalism and biography. Worse, he has become the victim of his own success, for the wealth that it has brought him has made him fair game in the real world, or what Citrine calls the 'moronic inferno'. This reality comes as something of a shock to Citrine, because it makes him reconsider the place of culture in the world outside. As an intellectual he has thought of himself as living a higher life of the mind, with a mission to discover and pass on truth to the world (his great project is to write a history of boredom). But his ability to adhere to the higher values of the inner life is put to a severe test by what he learns about the strange connections between culture and money, for the outer world is defiantly materialist, with no interest in the meaning of literary culture. It is a world of expensive objects, inhabited by predatory lawyers and crooked businessmen, by operators and racketeers, by upwardly-mobile gangsters who want to talk about Ardrey and Lorenz, by sharks and cannibals.

Much of the novel's comic energy is to be found amongst the inhabitants of the moronic inferno. Citrine's would-be guide through this 'hell' is Rinaldo Cantabile, a small-time crook with pretensions to culture (his wife is writing a thesis on Humboldt) who wrecks Citrine's Mercedes with a baseball bat because Citrine reneged on a debt. Cantabile is another of Bellow's reality instructors; taking pity on what he sees as Citrine's innocence he attempts to set himself up as the writer's protector in the Chicago world. Alec Szathmar, Citrine's crooked lawyer friend, is a lecher and pimp who went through college claiming to be a poet. The loud, vulgar George Swiebel, self-styled expert on the underworld, is identified in South Chicago with 'Bohemia and the Arts, with creativity, with imagination' (Ch. 5). The charming but feckless Pierre Thaxter, parasite and secret agent, who gets Citrine involved in the financial disaster of *The Ark*, has a project to turn artists into commodities for tourists. The moronic inferno plays hell with culture.

Although the moronic inferno is everywhere, Bellow embodies it specifically in Chicago. Chicago, says Citrine, 'with its gigantesque outer life contained the whole problem of poetry and the inner life in America' (Ch. 2). In his interview with Jo Brans Bellow said 'In Chicago it's very hard to find people to talk literature to. You find them at the university, and that's the long and the short of the thing. There is no literary culture in the United States'.[57] But Chicago was founded for material reasons and it was founded on blood, on the butchery of the stockyards and gangsterism. This accounts for the novel's insistent equation of money with blood, and especially its images of cannibalism and vampirism. The most obvious of these are related to the manner in which his ex-wife and her lawyers are draining away his money. The novel draws our attention more than once to Denise's 'sharp, sibylline' teeth. 'That crazy broad won't be satisfied until she's got your liver in her deepfreeze' Citrine's brother Julius tells him (Ch. 31). Her lawyer, Pinsker, is nicknamed 'Cannibal', characterized by Cantabile as a 'man-eating kike': 'He'll chop up your liver with egg and onion' (Ch.18). It is natural, in this context, that Citrine should see *Von Trench*, the source of his money, as 'the blood-scent that attracted the sharks of Chicago' (Ch. 18). For Humboldt, resentful at the play's success, the blood is *his* blood; his claim that Citrine used him for the character of Von Trench is, metaphorically speaking, a claim to have been cannibalized, and his response is ironically appropriate: he uses the cheque that Citrine had given him as a sign of their blood-brotherhood to withdraw money from Citrine's bank, thus drawing blood from him.

In the moronic inferno, then, money is blood, is life. It is also, by extension, love. Citrine's brother Julius (constantly depicted trying to satisfy his voracious appetites), when faced with the intensity of Citrine's love, can only express his own feelings by offering to invest money for him. Renata Koffritz gives Citrine both erotic and aesthetic satisfaction (she is another of the sexy dream women that Bellow likes to give to his heroes), but Citrine, in his fifties, is not really deluded about the source of her interest in him, and the demands of her sexual energy are a reminder to him of his own mortality. It is small wonder that he attempts to escape from this ethical confusion through his meditations.

In his meditations on his own life Citrine tries to retrieve moments of solace from the past, from those, now dead, whom he has loved. Apart from Humboldt, these include his parents and other figures from his childhood, and Demmie Vonghel, a woman with whom he was deeply in love, who was killed in an air crash. His attempts to resurrect his loved dead in this way make him consider the possibility that death is not final, and he becomes preoccupied with the idea of escape. The subject of one of his books is the great escape artist Harry Houdini, who 'defied all forms of restraint and confinement, including the grave. . . . They buried him and he escaped' (Ch. 35). But Houdini was really only an illusionist, and even he could not escape from the final fact of death. Citrine seeks a different understanding of death and the persistence of the spirit in the anthroposophical teachings of Rudolf Steiner. Steiner, a nineteenth-century occultist, developed a doctrine that taught that there is a spirit world that can be known through scientific enquiry. Bellow had at the time an interest in Steiner (as he had earlier been

interested in Reich), and his use of Steiner's ideas in a realistic
novel provoked some critical hostility, for, as Citrine points out, 'In
the learned world anthroposophy was not respectable' (Ch. 23).
Bellow felt obliged to reply to such criticism:

> I think people were confused by seeing Rudolf Steiner's work
> pop up in a novel a good part of which was comic in intent. I do
> admit to being intrigued with Steiner. I do not know enough to
> call myself a Steinerian. . . . I think it enough now to say that
> Rudolf Steiner had a great vision and was a powerful poet as well
> as philosopher and scientist.[58]

Bellow is characteristically evasive here on the question of how
seriously he took Steiner's ideas, but we do not have to assume that
they are being offered in *Humboldt's Gift* as 'truth'; rather they are
part of Citrine's meditative escape from the moronic inferno,
giving him the same kind of imaginative consolation as his memories of Humboldt.

Citrine's revulsion from American materialism, his attempt to
escape into some kind of higher spiritual truth, is understandable,
but in the end it is the result of a failure of perspective. He sees the
separation between mind and body rather than their interconnec-
tions. So, he insists on thinking of his mistress Renata as a work of
art, when much of the evidence suggests that she is a 'gross tough
broad' (Ch. 6). He himself, for all his intellectual levitation, his
yearnings of the spirit, is very much a creature of the flesh, an
overdressed chaser, often ludicrous. In his account of Humboldt
he attempts to reconcile the downward pull with the upward: 'He
was fine as well as thick, heavy but also light, and his face was both
pale and dark' and, most perceptively, 'Below, shuffling comedy;
above, princeliness and dignity' (Ch. 2). This is the tragi-comic
business of life: the princely dignity of the mind is inextricable
from the shuffling comedy of the body, and to try to deny it leads
to the unease with the world that Citrine suffers.

At the end of the novel Citrine seems to have gone some way
towards bridging the gap and accepting his own complicity in the
moronic inferno. It is his sensualist enjoyment of the rewards of his
success that has created his unease, but now his 'romance with
wealth' is over. He has been abandoned by Renata, who claims that
she can no longer tolerate his struggle to escape from the fact that
death is death, but who has probably left him because he is going

broke. His fortunes, however, are somewhat repaired by the success of the film *Caldofreddo* (a film, significantly, about cannibalism, and plagiarized – that is, cannibalized – from a story that he and Humboldt had written years before). He sees the irony of the fact that Humboldt, who only wanted to work on higher things, should have his reputation re-made by what Citrine calls 'capers' – by a film, a commodity, a product not of an individual mind but of a business collaboration, and that the millions to whom the film appeals misunderstand it. In the novel's final scene, standing in the graveyard where Humboldt has been re-buried, he is still thinking about how to escape the grave, but then admits, 'One didn't, didn't, didn't! You stayed, you stayed!' It is a tragic fact, but the recognition of it doesn't lead to despair. The spring flower growing in the graveyard is a sign of natural persistence, and Citrine's final comment, 'I'm a city boy myself', associates him with Chicago, with the moronic inferno, but also, affirmatively, with community.

5

Novels of the Eighties

Saul Bellow received the Nobel Prize for Literature in 1976. Few American authors have been awarded the Nobel Prize and those who received it generally saw it as a sign that their best creative days were ended. Bellow himself noted of John Steinbeck 'how burdened he was by the Nobel Prize. He felt that he had to give a better account of himself than he had done'.[59] It may have been this sense that the prize is somehow a blight on the career of a writer that made Bellow cautious about his fiction; at any rate, his next novel, *The Dean's December*, did not appear until 1982, and it was sufficiently lacking in those elements that were considered to be characteristic of Bellow at his best to make many critics wonder whether he had, indeed, gone into a decline, a speculation summed up by the judgement of Harold Bloom: 'Bellow's Alexander [sic] Corde tells us that "Chicago wasn't Chicago anymore." What *The Dean's December* truly tells us is that "Bellow wasn't Bellow anymore," in this book anyway'.[60] The real Bellow, for Bloom, is a writer of the comic grotesque, and *The Dean's December*, as its title implies, is a wintry tale indeed, an account of a mind obsessed by a vision of a decayed world, with very little comedy of any sort.

The problem may, of course, lie in the false expectations of the critics rather than in any failure of Bellow's art, for it appears that for some time Bellow had been thinking about more direct, non-fictional expression of his political and cultural preoccupations. In 1976 he had published *To Jerusalem and Back: A Personal Account*. Although this is an unashamedly pro-Israeli book, and consequently fails fully to engage all the complexities of the issues it raises, it has at its centre a series of questions that are closely connected to the concerns of his fictions, questions about survival in a world that seems to be disintegrating, about the loss of moral authority of the West, and about Bellow's own sense of identity as American and Jew. Bellow is deeply involved with the fate of Israel, and his journey there was a journey into his own history. 'It is my childhood revisited', he says in the book's opening paragraph, as he looks at a group of Hasidim who are also on a pilgrimage to Jerusalem. His own journey was to Jerusalem and back, however, and it ended in Chicago, 'this huge, filthy, brilliant, and mean city'.[61] There Bellow began work on another personal account, this time of Chicago itself, but found that the non-fictional treatment of the material was inadequate: 'the very language you have to use as a journalist works against the true material'.[62] Much of this material, looking for its 'poetic' truth, found its way into *The Dean's December*.

Bellow has always been willing to mine his own autobiography for stuff for his fictions, and as we have seen, this has often encouraged critics to see his protagonists as mouthpieces for their author. In the case of *The Dean's December*, even critics who are generally sympathetic towards Bellow's work have noted in the book what they see as an excessive amount of the author's own unmediated opinion, along with a loss of interest or a weariness about the activity of creating fiction.[63] It is certainly true that many of Albert Corde's concerns are Bellow's own, and that their polemical edge is unblunted by the comic undercutting that complicates the attitude of most of his earlier novels. It also appears, however, that Bellow has tried to distance himself from his protagonist by making him a gentile American of wealthy French-Irish extraction. The character who now embodies Bellow's own experience, the self-taught Jewish intellectual who with his own mental energy raised himself out of the Chicago slums to the status of international pundit, is Corde's childhood friend and rival Dewey Spangler who is, perhaps not incidentally, treated comically. But even though Corde presents himself and his opinions with great seriousness the reader is not, I think, intended to accept him or his views uncritically, for what we have here is a character who is too deeply absorbed by his own vision of the world to realize that it might be incomplete or distorted. Once again, by switching back and forth between first- and third-person, Bellow has presented a narrative perspective that is not to be trusted.

Most of the action of *The Dean's December* takes place in Bucharest during a few days around Christmas. The Dean of the novel's title, Albert Corde, is there with his wife Minna, a Rumanian-born astronomer who defected to America twenty years before, to visit Minna's dying mother Valeria Raresh. Valeria had been Minister of Health thirty years earlier, but had fallen from grace with the Communist Party. Now, a cruel and unforgiving bureaucracy, represented by a 'whiplash Colonel' of the secret police, is using its power to prevent her daughter from visiting her in the hospital. The energies of Corde and Minna are mainly expended on a struggle with this bureaucracy, as they try first to arrange to see Valeria and then, after her death, to give her a dignified funeral. During this time Corde lives in Valeria's decaying apartment, visited by relatives and well-wishers, and observes the bleak existence of the inmates of what he calls a 'penitentiary society', grubbing for even the most basic material necessities, and silenced by fear of wiretappers and informers. His distaste for this grim place is aggravated by his anxieties about Minna, who he fears may still be subject to Rumanian law.

These immediate concerns are not Corde's only worries, however. Once a successful journalist, he gave up the profession because of what he saw as a lack of poetry in it and entered the academic world. He had wanted to get back to the reading and ideas that had inspired him in his youth, and he is now Professor of Journalism and Dean at a Chicago college. As both journalist and Dean, however, he has recently brought to himself unwelcome and controversial attention. He wrote some articles about Chicago for *Harper's* magazine which focused on what Corde identified as an underclass, the blacks whose lives are circumscribed by slums and barren public housing projects, by hospitals, detoxification centres and prisons, and are defined by poverty, violence and hopelessness. Corde blamed this state of affairs upon the callousness of Chicago politicians, the backroom dealing that made corruption and racism endemic in the city. These articles created much resentment against him, but as if that were not enough he also became involved in another set of events with racial overtones. A student at his college, Rick Lester, was killed in a fall from his apartment window. As Dean, Corde felt it his duty to investigate the death, and largely because of his efforts a thief and a prostitute, both black, were charged with Lester's murder. However, Corde's nephew Mason, a campus activist, took up the cause of the thief, Lucas Ebry, claiming that the charges were racially motivated. Worse still, Corde's cousin Max Detillion, a lawyer whose skills are mainly used to get publicity for himself, and who for various reasons hates Corde, was engaged to defend Ebry. Corde is now awaiting the outcome of the trial, for his future depends upon it.

Through the imperatives of his own moral fervour he has found himself in a peculiarly ironic position where, having accused Chicago of racism, he is himself the target of the same accusation. Corde's activities have deeply embarrassed his college, and its Provost, Alec Witt, is clearly waiting for an opportunity to get rid of him.

Corde obviously has much to think about, and *The Dean's December* is built around his ruminations about the way in which two societies so widely separated have imposed such crushing burdens upon the spirit of their inhabitants. The construction of the novel is complex. Little happens in the immediate present, and many of the events come to us through a series of flashbacks that take place in the Dean's memory. He remembers his early meetings with Valeria and her sister Gigi, and their suspicion of him as a suitable husband for Minna because of his reputation as a womanizer. He remembers especially Valeria's visits to London, her touching pleasure in her brief freedom. Her delight in buying frivolous luxuries there has its ironic explanation in the long queues at home for black market grapes and bad steak. The texture of Bucharest life is built out of these memories, out of a few halting conversations Corde has with Rumanian visitors, and from observations he makes when he occasionally ventures out of the apartment. Chicago, of course, is much more completely a part of Corde's consciousness, and it is presented to the reader through recollections prompted by telephone calls and packages of letters from home, and by his reconstruction, as he re-reads his *Harper's* articles, of the encounters that led to their writing. He tries to make sense of his experience, to bridge the gap between the Western city and the East European capital, in a series of conversations with his wife, with the American ambassador, who tries to help him deal with Rumanian bureaucracy, with Vlada Voynich, a Rumanian scientist who now lives in America but is visiting Rumania, and, most importantly, with Dewey Spangler, a boyhood friend who is now a famous international journalist.

The reader who casts his mind back to Bellow's first novel will at once note the similarity of the Dean's situation to Joseph's. Joseph's alienation was self-imposed; his sense of his own powerlessness made him seek a conscious isolation from others that left him alone in his room with his own increasingly distorted thoughts. Corde's situation is not of his own choosing, but he is largely isolated from those who visit Valeria's apartment by his inability to speak their language, and aware of his impotence in a society in which he is literally 'alien'. He consequently spends much of his time as Joseph did, brooding alone in a dingy room looking out on to a depressing cityscape. The Dean too is a 'dangling man', suspended between two worlds as he seeks a meaning for human history, and putting a misplaced faith in the certainty of his own understanding.

Corde's 'dangling' extends beyond the immediate conditions of his situation in Bucharest, however, for it has become the condition of his life. His career as a journalist had begun in a spectacular manner: as a young soldier in Europe near the end of the war he had, through personal contacts, been able to see at first hand the great Western leaders, Churchill, Stalin and Truman, and had written a brilliant account of the Potsdam Conference for *The New Yorker*. Upon this foundation he had built a successful career as a journalist, based in Paris. He had become convinced, however, that the kinds of truth that the journalist must deal in are superficial, at their best no more than 'high-grade intellectual plush', as he says of the work of his friend Spangler (Ch. 5). Seeking something deeper, in what he calls poetry and philosophy, he moved back to Chicago and entered the academic world, but found little poetry there either. Now he feels he is displaced, in the wrong game: 'He was something of a stand-in, a journalist passing for a dean' (Ch. 3). His fervour for what he calls 'a moral life' (Ch. 4) urged him to a brief return to journalism, but his articles about Chicago mixed a violent antagonism with obscurity of thought and language – philosophy and poetry – that mystified and angered his readers. As with his involvement with the Ebry case, his desire to uncover truth, to do the right thing, somehow led him to disaster.

Corde's problem is that he is unable to find the right tone for dealing with the world; in his sister's view he has 'a minimum of common ground with the people about him' (Ch. 3). He is an essentially impractical man who believes he has a grasp on some higher truth, some mystical essence beyond the surface of things. He has, we are told, 'the brown gaze of an intricate mind of an absent, probably dreamy tendency' (Ch. 1), and we may remember that Herzog too was dreamy, and let the sharpies clean him out. The sharpies are certainly after Corde: his cousin Detillion has already cleaned him out, and tough men, realists like his late brother-in-law Zaehner and the Provost Witt, have nothing but contempt for what Zaehner calls 'this dud dean' (Ch. 4). Even Dewey Spangler sees in Corde an apparent need to self-destruct.

But as with so many of Bellow's heroes, what makes Corde valuable is also what causes his problems – his uncompromising opposition to these reality instructors or pragmatists, his refusal to be limited by what they see as truth. For what Corde wants to say, insists on saying, is that there is evil in the world.

The Dean's December presents Bellow's angriest, most horrified version of a modern world on the edge of apocalypse, approached only by what we saw on Mr Sammler's planet. America as represented here by Chicago is an urban hell, a derelict society about to sink into the vast sewer, the *cloaca maxima* beneath it. Corde thinks of it as a moronic inferno, the phrase echoing from *Humboldt's Gift*, but there is nothing of Citrine's comic world in this inferno. The Chicago slums are inhabited by a chaotic army, seen by Corde as an underclass: 'blacks, Koreans, East Indians, Chippewas, Thais and hillbillies, squad cars, ambulances, firefighters, thrift shops, drug hustlers, lousy bars, alley filth' (Ch. 16). The threat of violence is everywhere, bursting out of repressed lives, as rape and robbery escalate into murder. The hopelessness of this infernal Chicago and the quality of Corde's response to it are brilliantly caught in an account of his visit to a detoxification centre:

> The one remaining landmark was the abandoned Englewood Station – huge blocks of sandstone set deep, deep in the street, a kind of mortuary isolation, no travellers now, no passenger trains. A dirty snow brocade over the empty lots, and black men keeping warm at oil-drum bonfires. All this – low sky, wind, weeds, skeletons, ruin – went to Corde's nerves, his 'Chicago wiring system,' with peculiar effect. . . . He parked and got out of the car feeling the lack of almost everything you needed, humanly. Christ, the human curve had sunk down to base level, had gone beneath it. If there was another world, this was the time for it to show itself. The visible one didn't bear looking at.
>
> (Ch. 9)

The passage illustrates beautifully the relationship between landscape and vision in the novel: what Corde sees is a measure for evaluating the world.

The barrenness of this landscape of poverty is matched by the spiritual barrenness of the city's rich and powerful, the Chicago insiders. Corde thinks of Chicago as the 'contempt center of the U.S.A' (Ch. 3), and as such its best representative is his late brother-in-law Morton Zaehner. Zaehner's contempt is for what he sees as Corde's ivory-tower escapism, his failure to understand the 'real' Chicago, but Zaehner's own realism is actually a bullying, arrogant pragmatism that Corde describes as 'brutal'. The Provost of Corde's college, Alec Witt, is described in similar terms: 'he was a rough Chicago man; his neck, his chest, told you that, not big but brutal, definitely' (Ch. 3), and his attitude to Corde is similar to Zaehner's. Even Dewey Spangler, that figure of international sophistication (and another Spirit of Alternatives, one of those alter-ego figures that shadow so many of Bellow's heroes), owes his success to a predator's view of the world, an ability to manipulate the 'cultural capital' of his early intellectual education into a career, and it is his predatory instinct that finally makes him destroy the career of his old friend and rival.

This Chicago contempt-attitude is to do with the loss of a sense of what is properly to be valued. The novel is haunted by a line from Shelley's sonnet 'England in 1819' about the loss of moral authority of the 'old mad blind despised and dying king' George III. The significance for Bellow here of Shelley's bitter poem is clear, with its rendering of a divided society with rulers who can 'neither see, nor feel, nor know', and a people 'starved and stabbed in the untilled field'. The moral blindness of those who neither see nor feel nor know is presented in the scene, at once comic and appalling, in which Corde attends a party that he discovers is for a dog. This scene takes on an almost symbolic significance. In a luxurious apartment high above the starved and stabbed in the wrecked Chicago streets a group of wealthy socialites give presents and sing 'Happy Birthday' to a Great Dane that becomes, for Corde, the Great Beast of the Apocalypse, a final sign of the catastrophe awaiting this 'all-but-derelict civilization' (Ch. 17).

Chicago is, of course, here as everywhere, metonymic for America, and the book is about the country's loss of direction, its failure to maintain its historical position of moral leadership. Corde in his articles (like Bellow in his novel) seeks 'to prevent the American idea from being pounded into dust altogether' (Ch. 5). In struggling to define that idea, he keeps coming back to the word 'decency'. His interest in the murdered Rick Lester arises from his conviction that the young man was essentially good, trying to live a 'decently organized' life (Ch. 3). Lester's widow is 'a good young woman' with 'decent instincts' (Ch. 3). Rufus Ridpath, one of the two black heroes that Corde finds in his investigation of the

Chicago underclass, is 'a decent, intelligent public servant' (Ch. 3). When Corde is rejecting a suggestion that his wife might have used dishonest means to visit her dying mother he says 'That would be completely out of character. She's an unusually . . .' (Ch. 4). He doesn't finish his sentence, but we can be sure he would have said 'decent woman'. 'Decency' seems to imply a degree of altruism and of self-control, and, more important, a sense that there are some things that are absolutely wrong. In his discussion with the U.S. Ambassador in Bucharest Corde talks about the way in which a scale of 'evil' has developed; 'A is bad, but B is worse and C is worse still. When you reach N, unspeakable evil, A becomes trivial' (Ch. 4). He is talking about the repressive Rumanian regime, but the relativism he is defining is what has undermined the American idea, and he wants to insist on a recognition that A's badness is not made trivial by the fact that other things are worse. Men have a responsibility to do right. It is this belief that makes him reluctant to accept the scientist Sam Beech's theory that lead poisoning is the cause of the decline of civilization, for this is also a theory that denies human responsibility, proposing purely material causes of evil.

In his articles Corde ruminates on how American 'freedom' has helped bring about the disappearance of decency. In Rumania he finds a people who, while living in a 'penitentiary society', deprived and persecuted, have managed to remain decent. Spangler defines very well the texture of life in this socialist prison: 'a miserable damn comfortless life, and scary as well as boring' (Ch. 5). The genteel poverty of the society gathered around Corde's mother-in-law is, no doubt about it, deeply pathetic. Living amongst the faded reminders of a better past, the Bucharest people struggle to maintain their dignity through a pretence that things are not really as bad as they seem: their coffee, even if dominated by chicory, is Turkish; their bric-a-brac and trinkets may be national treasures. Despite the pathos, however, they live with integrity, lives of mutual dependence in which even the activities of spies and informers can be accepted as part of the necessary accommodation to life. It is difficult not to conclude that Bellow sees this positive decency as arising from the feminine energies of the society.

The Chicago we see in *The Dean's December* is firmly male-dominated, and Chicago brutality is so distinctly masculine that even the prostitute Riggie Hines, who was involved in the killing of Rick Lester, is described as being man-like. In Bucharest, the

oppressors and predators are men (the Colonel, the 'savage' Dr
Gherea), but all that is positive and healing comes from the
'extended feminine hierarchy' (Ch. 4) that is dominated by 'great
Valeria'. It is here, in this world of women, that Corde's own testing
takes place, for he has to prove his worth to Valeria. Corde, the
novel tells us, has a reputation as a swinger. We have to take this on
faith, as no evidence is provided – unlike Herzog and Charlie
Citrine, Corde is not pursued and harried by women from his past.
Because of this reputation, however, Valeria has had doubts about
Corde's suitability as a husband for her daughter Minna, even
though Corde is, he insists, 'by the strictest marital standards
decent, mature, intelligent, responsible, an excellent husband'
(Ch. 6). Indeed, if we exclude Leventhal of *The Victim*, whose wife
Mary hardly exists in that novel, Corde is the first of Bellow's
protagonists to have a more-or-less untroubled relationship with a
woman. Others have been motivated by lust, or by a vanity that is
flattered by the possession of a beautiful woman, but there is a
mutuality in the relationship between Corde and Minna that is new
in Bellow's work.

Minna is a rather shadowy figure, but this may be because of
Corde's own misconceptions about her. He sees her concern with
the stars as keeping her detached from mundane affairs, and so he
takes pride in explaining things to her (he appears not to see that
there is something comic in this dreamy dean explaining things to
the unworldly Minna). But her angry response to him when he
tries to analyse her feelings about her dead mother, that she is tired
of hearing his lectures, seems to indicate that she has allowed him
this demonstration of superior masculine understanding only to
humour him, while his conviction that she is unworldly is a means
of avoiding excessive intimacy with her. Still, his need to justify
himself to the female principle as embodied in Valeria (who sees in
him all the possibilities of Western corruption) is part of Corde's
own crisis in the book. This explains the violent power of the
moment when he tells her that he loves her.

The other part of his personal crisis that is concerned with
Valeria is his need to come to terms with death. His apocalyptic
visions allow him to imagine the death of the race, but this is not the
same as understanding personal death. As with other Bellow
heroes before him, especially Mr Sammler, Corde's experience of
the death of a loved one, as he himself sees, is a kind of rehearsal
for his own death. His descent from the icy dome of the cremator-

ium to the fiery vault beneath it is rendered with a terrible immediacy that makes the movement symbolic, and later he imagines the moment of her body's dissolution in a manner too vivid for it not to be a rehearsal of the dissolution of his own:

> At this very instant Valeria might be going into the fire, the roaring furnace which took off her hair, the silk scarf, grabbed away the green suit, melted the chased silver buttons, consumed the skin, flashed away the fat, blew up the organs, reached the bones, bore down on the skull – that refining fire, a ball of raging gold, a tiny sun, a star. (Ch. 12)

Corde reprises this movement outward to the stars at the end of the novel, when he is in another icy dome in the observatory at Mount Palomar. Looking out at the mystery of infinite space he sees for a moment the possibility of freedom, and is reluctant to return to earth.

In many ways this is a novel of exhaustion, and it is not surprising that, beset by intimations of approaching apocalypse and a growing intimacy with the idea of his own death, Corde frequently echoes the voice of the poet W. B. Yeats. Confronted by his nephew Mason, a representative of the relativist perspective of youth, Corde looks at his clock and sees the 'long-legged fly' (Ch. 3) which in Yeats's poem of that title represents the mind of Caesar considering how civilization might be saved. He thinks of the masses in the black underclasses as 'dying generations' (Ch. 12), the phrase borrowed from 'Sailing to Byzantium', a poem in which the aged scarecrow Yeats attempts to escape, through art and intellect, from the limiting world of youthful sensuality (this poem is also invoked by Spangler as a major part of his education). Most significant of all are the echoes of 'The Second Coming'. In this poem Yeats has a vision of a civilization tearing away from its centre, whirling outward in ever increasing circles to a moment of explosion in which destruction will engulf the world. Corde sees the masses of Chicago, brutalized into criminality, as living 'whirling lives' (Ch. 8), spinning outward to an explosion; and, writing about them, he becomes himself a whirling soul, a part of the anarchy loosed upon the world (Ch. 10).

The Dean's December is, without question, a bleak book. It is also a deeply serious book, looking with uncompromising honesty at what Bellow takes to be the current state of America, and seeing very little to be optimistic about. This may account for the negative response to the book of many reviewers, who saw in Corde's numerous jeremiads no more than an ill-fitting mask for Bellow's own polemics. Corde is not a simple surrogate for Bellow, and we are invited to look at him with some irony. Still, what is on his mind is what is on Bellow's mind, and we are forced to examine some fearful things. At one point, Corde recalls a complaint of Rilke, that he was unable to find an adequate attitude to the things and the people around him (Ch. 4), and finds himself with the same problem. 'There's nothing too rum to be true' is a refrain that runs through the book, and the implied question is: What attitude should we take to these rum things? The novel replies that we cannot find an adequate attitude, but this does not absolve us from the duty of looking squarely at what is monstrous, and *The Dean's December* does precisely that.

Bellow's next extended piece of fiction, the novel *More Die of Heartbreak*, appeared in 1987. Like Albert Corde in Bucharest, the narrator of *More Die of Heartbreak* is an expatriate looking at an alien world that appears to him confused and fallen. Kenneth Trachtenberg was born and raised in Paris. His American father, a notable seducer of women, had himself chosen to live as an expatriate in France, where he had known such literary figures as Malraux and Queneau and received as a frequent dinner guest the Hegelian philosopher Alexandre Kojeve. Kenneth had consequently developed a love for large ideas, and also for Russian thought and literature. Seeking to understand the contemporary world, he rejected both the lessons offered by his father's philandering and the Parisian intellectual milieu, and emigrated to America because, as he tells us, 'that's where the action is now – the real modern action' (Ch. 2). He also wanted to become the disciple of his uncle, the famous American botanist Benn Crader, from whose deep perceptions of the nature of things (what Kenneth calls his 'magics') he hoped to learn. But Benn, at home with heavyweight thought and capable of communing with plants, is as much an alien in the world of modern action – which here means sex, money and power – as his nephew is. Here again is the comedy of the other-worldly man, sensitive and thoughtful, haplessly taking on materialistic America, the domain of reality instructors and sharpies, of 'shrewdies' and 'pragmatists'.

Benn Crader is in his fifties, a professor of botany at a university in an unnamed Midwestern city, where Kenneth, some twenty years younger, teaches Russian literature. Because of their cerebral inclinations the two men have developed a relationship of strong inter-dependence: Kenneth sees his uncle as a mentor, in effect a spiritual father, but Benn equally needs Kenneth as a sounding-board for his ideas and feelings. The event that provokes Kenneth's narration is his uncle's disastrous decision to enter the world of modern desire and marry the brilliant and beautiful Matilda Layamon, daughter of a wealthy and greedy gynaecologist. Benn is a widower who has a history of flight from erotic entanglements, taking refuge in lecture tours in Brazil or Japan, but in this case he is convinced that he has found the right woman. As he discovers too late, however, Matilda is a committed materialist. She has planned a future for herself as a society hostess, and she sees Benn largely as an ornament, an object whose function will be to attract desirable guests through the exotic pull of his reputation as a scientist. Worse than this, her father Dr Layamon wants to use Benn to extort millions of dollars out of Benn's uncle, Harold Vilitzer, a ruthless politician who many years ago had cheated Benn and his sister (Kenneth's mother) in the sale of property that he knew to be worth a fortune. Not relishing either aspect of the future the Layamons have designed for him, Benn takes flight once again, this time on a scientific expedition to the North Pole where, amongst the lichens that somehow manage to survive in the icy wastes, he will regenerate the bonds with the vegetable world that he betrayed in his foray into the world of human relationships.

As Kenneth relates this story he reveals much of his own, which has interesting similarities. One of the causes of his decision to leave France was his father's erotic virtuosity, which, although Kenneth rejected it as a model for his own life, apparently gave him doubts about his own sexual adequacy. These doubts seem to be confirmed by the unsatisfactory nature of the relationship in which he finds himself. He is in love with Treckie Sterling (by whom he has a daughter), but she refuses to marry him, apparently preferring more 'physical' men like Ronald, the ski-instructor with whom she is now living. He becomes the unwilling object of the attentions of Treckie's mother, who proposes marriage to him, and he is also more gently pursued by the estimable but plain Dita Schwartz, a one-time student of his. His own story reaches a climax when he decides to fly to Seattle to confront Treckie, imagining himself doing violence to Ronald. But after ripping up her bedding and wrecking her bathroom he recognizes the melodrama of his situation (like Herzog watching Gersbach through the window of another bathroom) and acknowledges that he isn't what Treckie has been looking for. Dita Schwartz isn't what *he* has been looking for, but he returns to her with a greater understanding of the true worth, the kindness and love, that this plain woman represents – a triumph of sorts.

These events are presented in a narrative which in its indirections and circlings takes in also, amongst many other things, Benn's childhood, Kenneth's education, Benn's experiences at a Japanese strip-tease show and a parole-board hearing of a rape case, and Kenneth's visit with his mother who is a relief worker in East Africa. It presents film criticism, of Hitchcock's *Psycho* and Wim Wenders' *The American Friend*, and it gives us information about plant morphology, Russian philosophy and the mystical writings of Swedenborg. These are not digressions because they are all connected to the novel's central issues, but they also indicate the quality of the mind that is represented by the narrative voice, a voice which, in a manner characteristic of Bellow, combines the racy and the cerebral. There are, of course, problems with this; as with other Bellow monologists the excesses of garrulity may be blamed on the novelist rather than the narrator, and at least one reviewer found the novel 'phenomenally dull'.[64] I think, however, we have to see these excesses as defining areas of Kenneth's character, which contains no small degree of intellectual smugness.

As the synopsis indicates, *More Die of Heartbreak* is about love, or, rather, it is about what has happened to love at the moment in history that is defined by the America of the novel, which Kenneth calls variously the 'posthistorical age', the 'posthuman age' and the 'age of desire'. Modern Western culture has laid such emphasis on materialism that all higher human powers are despised. In the terms of the novel, human need and aspiration have been channelled into the erotic, and while the erotic itself has shrunk to an animal appetite, men and women still perceive erotic failure as human failure. But as Kenneth sees it even erotic success is problematic, for what begins in the material ends in the material, which is why he rejects his father as a mentor: 'The premise of his eroticism was mortality. The sex embrace was death-flavoured' (Ch. 2). Erotic love is now mere self-gratification, and as such it is destructive of the self and careless of its object. The poet William Blake (who figures frequently in this novel) wrote of self-centred love in 'The Clod and the Pebble':

Love seeketh only Self to please,
To bind another to its delight,
Joys in another's loss of ease,
And builds a Hell in Heaven's despite.

This is what Matilda Layamon would do to Benn, turning him into a kind of highbrow tourist attraction for her dinner guests, but the novel provides a more chilling image of the way in which self-pleasing 'love' abuses another in Benn's account of the parole hearing about the rape of Danae Cusper. After his violent act of self-gratification the rapist used a broken bottle to cut the word 'LOV' into the girl's abdomen. This cynical mutation of love into 'LOV' corresponds to the mystical appearance of a small glacier in each human breast, described to Kenneth by his first Russian teacher, M. Yermelov. The glacier can only be melted by the warmth of human love, which men now resist.

The repression of human need into a simple erotic imperative is destroying us all. Benn's flight to Brazil is precipitated by the attentions of Della Bedell, a lady who lives in his apartment building. Plain, short and fat, she cannot generate desire in another; Benn goes to bed with her almost accidentally, and when later he avoids her she puts notes in his mailbox: 'What am I supposed to do with my sexuality?' The situation is farcical, yet it reveals the despair of the erotic failure. While Benn is in Brazil Della dies of a cardiac arrest, for which he blames himself: 'I see her suffocated by swollen longings'. It is this idea that prompts him to respond to a journalist who asks about the radiation level in plants with the statement that provides the novel with its title: 'I think more people die of heartbreak than of radiation' (Ch. 3). This is not a remark intended to dismiss or minimize the threat of radiation, but Benn's point appears to be that a preoccupation with material destruction has made us neglect the far more widespread spiritual destruction that results from the disappearance of love. Della's story has its counterpart in that of Dita Schwartz who, also suffering from swollen longings, undergoes the extreme physical pain of a medical treatment that amounts to self-laceration in an effort to make herself erotically desirable for Kenneth.

As Kenneth sees it, this confusion about love and desire arises because the world is suffering from a division of the physical from the spiritual, and he seeks for himself a higher mode of living. As he says, 'you have no reason to exist unless you believe you can make your life a turning point. A turning point for everybody – for humankind' (Ch. 2). This may seem a grandiose view to hold of the significance of one's own existence but in Kenneth's case it is an insistence on an ethical need, for his life to set a pattern that goes against the current of contemporary circumstances. The experience of the novel seems to suggest that it is impossible to live in the world without being contaminated by it, unless you can be, like Benn, 'a man capable of living fully in isolation from the life of his time' (Ch. 9). Kenneth sees Benn quite seriously as a genius, a man close to becoming a 'Citizen of Eternity', ranking with the likes of Moses, Odysseus, the Prophets, Socrates, Mozart, Pushkin and Blake. Benn's genius lies in his peculiar, even transcendent, ability to see into the lives of plants. It is represented literally in terms of vision: the oddity of Benn's eyes is frequently stressed as Kenneth describes them as being like a figure eight turned on its side, producing a disturbing gaze 'when you felt the power of *looking* turned on you' (Ch. 1). The power of looking, of a vision that goes beyond surfaces, beyond the material, is also indicated metaphorically here, for the tilted figure eight is the sign for infinity. Benn's preternatural vision is what Kenneth refers to as his 'magics'; his eyes are receptive, taking in what others do not see, which in itself generates that superiority that makes him a candidate for Eternal Citizenship: 'Man is what he sees' (Ch. 1). Kenneth's own ambition is to go beyond Benn, to learn from his uncle's magics to bring to the human world the vision that Benn brings to plant life. This is how he will make his own life a turning point for mankind.

This is all serious stuff, but the novel is, nevertheless, comic. Benn's ability to be in tune with natural harmonies might in this context be defined as 'love', and we should note the consolation he receives from contact with a Christmas tree during his wedding ceremony. He falls into the material world of 'LOV' when be becomes attached to Matilda Layamon, and the comedy arises from his struggles to understand this world (which he entered because he thought that he did understand it) and then to free himself from it. Matilda is a woman of high intelligence, though this is exhibited in an interest in literary fascists. Her family lives a life-style of opulence and doubtful taste mainly intended to advertise its wealth, and Matilda, with her peculiar exotic and brittle kind of beauty, a 'glittering, nervous, French-Midwestern woman' (Ch. 4), fits well amongst the furnishings. The ambiguity of the Layamon household is underlined by Dr Layamon's attitude to both his wealth and his daughter, veering between boasting and virulent criticism. It is also emphasized by the prurient interest of this gynaecologist in his daughter's sexual activities. He is one more in Bellow's line of fast-talking confidence tricksters, and the corruption (and danger) of his values, in comparison to Benn's clear vision or straight gaze, is implied by the distortion of sight indicated by his crooked spectacles: 'Doctor's eyeglasses didn't sit level and his glances, too, were skewed' (Ch. 4).

Benn becomes a part of this uncongenial household because, like everyone else, he needs love and thinks it can be found. He convinces himself that he has found it in Matilda by making an almost Platonic assumption that her physical beauty represents an inner beauty. Consequently he ignores his instincts, which send him warning messages about her. These come, comically, through the film *Psycho*, which Benn hates because it gains its effects through sensationalism and emotional manipulation and, worse still, because he feels himself respond to it. His identification of Matilda's shoulders with those of the mad killer in the film is one of a series of signs that disquiet him (like her sharp teeth, and her revelation of a streak of her father's coarseness in her), but that he nevertheless suppresses. His marriage, then, is a denial of his nature (and of nature) and it is presented in the novel as a fall.[65] The mythic overtones are made quite explicit. At the start of his narrative Kenneth imagines himself making a painting of his uncle in which Benn is pictured in a clearing in a forest partnered with a tree in the 'green seclusion' of what Kenneth calls a 'modern-dress Eden' (Ch. 1). The echo of the 'green shade' of Andrew Marvell's poem 'The Garden' is unmistakable; like Marvell's paradise, this one works because it has not been invaded by a woman:

> Such was that happy Garden-state
> While man there walked without a mate.
> . . .
> Two paradises 'twere in one,
> To live in Paradise alone.

As if trying to hold on to his Eden, Benn embraces the Christmas tree at the moment of his marriage, but he cannot prevent his own fall once he is in the midst of the fallen world of the Layamons, as is indicated by his failure to realize that Mrs Layamon's azalea, from which he has felt himself deriving comfort, is artificial. This loss of his botanist's vision, of his 'magics', is what precipitates his flight to polar isolation in the hope of learning to regain his paradise.

Although the novel's focus is on the degeneration of erotic love, this is only a part of a wider vision of a world altogether fallen, with no sense of the value of any human purpose. 'We've split things in two, dividing the physique from the mind' (Ch. 1), Kenneth says at one point, and this division is graphically illustrated by a sequence of scenes which focus the masculine gaze on the female sexual parts: at the Japanese strip-tease show; in the Maimonides Hospital, where Dr Layamon passes Benn off as a doctor to exhibit to him the private parts of old women; and at the hearing for the Cusper rape case. In each case sex has been turned into theatre to emphasize the separation between object and viewer; this exhibition is, to use Kenneth's word, 'literal' and, as he says, 'To be seen literally dries out one's humanity' (Ch. 3). The spectator of such literal exhibitions may be mystified or aroused, but he does not feel anything about the object that he abuses with his gaze. Benn is disturbed by all of these experiences, but most deeply so by the last, because it is here, in this arena of public and political showbiz, that he is forced to recognize that everything is as cynically debased as 'LOV': 'Crime, Punishment, Justice, Authority, were satirized in this hearing. Plus Penitence. Plus Truth' (Ch. 9).

In the middle of this mockery of values Benn confronts his Uncle Vilitzer, though his intention is not quite to go along with the Layamons' scheme to extort money from the old man. Vilitzer is a veteran political fixer who has amassed enormous wealth through corrupt dealings; many years ago he cheated Benn and his sister over a land deal from which he himself made a vast profit. In spite of this, Benn retains great affection for Vilitzer, who is lit by the nostalgic glow of Benn's memory of his childhood. Vilitzer responds to such feelings only with contempt, however, resisting even his son Fishl's desperate attempts to elicit a sign of love from him. The supreme realist and crooked fighter, who knows himself to be surrounded by crooks, his creed is that 'Where money is concerned, the operational word is *merciless*' or, as Kenneth glosses this, 'kinship is bullshit', and he is absolutely resistant to doing the right thing by his nephew. Now little more than a shell of a man, 'as light as an empty plastic egg carton' (Ch. 9), his heart taken over by a machine, Vilitzer is the novel's grimmest satirical picture of the dehumanizing effect of money. As such, he is appropriately associated with the construction of the Electronic Tower, a monument to power and money that throws a sinister shadow across the landscape (cityscape) of the novel.

The Electronic Tower works as a complex symbol, and it gains part of its effect from the way in which characters respond to it. Vilitzer's pride in his association with the Tower relates to its size and its function in generating money. Mrs Layamon, who can see it from her penthouse window, thinks it is 'an important piece of modern beauty' (Ch. 4). The rich and privileged can get from its summit a 'stunning view' of the urban devastation that has been caused in the pursuit of wealth, and in its phallic symbolism it relates to the novel's central concern with sexual self-gratification by implying the erotic attraction of money and power. To Benn, with his deeper vision, the Tower seems to take on a life of its own, at night moving closer to the penthouse building, as if threatening to crush it. He thinks of it as being like the *Titanic*, with immense potential for destruction. A more complex analysis, that indicates the danger of thinking through metaphor, is presented by Kenneth: 'Skyscrapers, as we all recognize, also express an aspiration towards freedom, a rising above. They may be filled with abominable enterprises, but they do transmit an idea of transcendence. Perhaps they mislead us or betray our hopes by an unsound analogy' (Ch. 9). In his appeal to general agreement ('as we all recognize') Kenneth implicates the reader as a probable victim of misread analogy, and we should turn back to Benn's image of the Tower-as-Titanic, suggesting sinking rather than rising.

Part of Benn's life has already been crushed beneath the weight of the Tower, for it is built upon the piece of land where Benn spent his childhood. 'My old life is lying under it' (Ch. 5), he says, and this is a significant statement because it is in his old life where Benn locates the source of emotional sustenance. He has a rosy vision of his childhood, and he continually reconstructs it in memory as a time of all-encompassing love and kindness. This is why he generates no resentment for Vilitzer, because he cannot detach the man he encounters at the Parole Board hearing from the Vilitzer of his childhood. Kenneth questions the accuracy of what Benn thinks he remembers, suggesting that his recollection of warm family affections is really a fairy tale, but even if it is a fairy tale Benn needs it, and he cannot cease loving Vilitzer. The difference between Benn and Vilitzer's son Fishl, who also deeply loves the old man, is that Fishl is pathetic because his love is unrequited, and he needs to be loved in return. Benn can love the old man without needing to have his love requited. But it is his need to love that tricks him into believing that Matilda is a deserving object.

At the end of the novel Benn is defeated. His understanding of love as altruism, as a sympathetic connection with another being, makes it impossible for him to continue to live amongst those for whom love is only egotistical self-gratification, but he is to a degree infected by the Layamon view, and is deeply wounded in the blunting of his responses to the vegetable world. It is appropriate that he decides to retire to the purifying cold of the North Pole (its effect like that of the Newfoundland snow where Henderson ends up or the icy dark of space that so tempts Albert Corde) and to the problem of the Arctic lichen which, like the human heart, is largely iced over but which can be revived with a little warmth. This seems a rather pessimistic ending, but as is usual with Bellow's novels, there are complicating factors which veil the novelist's intentions. These are to do first with the narrative voice and second with the relationship between the narrator and Benn.

For all his claims to intellectual clarity, Kenneth is a garrulous and disorderly narrator, the producer of a digressive structure for which he himself has to apologize. He exhibits a smug arrogance that is far from Benn's generosity of spirit, when he contemplates those 'shits' whom he considers to be inferior to himself, 'people of ordinary stunted imaginative powers' (Ch. 4). He visits his mother at her mission in East Africa and insists on regaling her with his views on the lost state of the world while failing to note that she is a living example of self-sacrificing love. Only late, and almost reluctantly, does he recognize the true inner beauty latent in Dita Schwartz. He treats his own unworldliness and that of his uncle as something that elevates them above the crowd – 'People like ourselves weren't part of the main enterprise' (Ch. 5) – but at the same time, despite his oft-proclaimed deference to Benn's 'magics', he can be somewhat condescending to aspects of his uncle's unworldliness. For example, he mocks Benn's attempt to express his love in terms of Edgar Allan Poe's poetry as naive, pointing out the immaturity of Poe's ideas of love, infatuated as he was with a woman locked in a state of permanent childhood, and he only belatedly recognizes that his own attraction to Treckie is to the child-woman in her. In sum, Kenneth admires himself rather more, perhaps, than we can admire him.

Still, Kenneth's love for Benn, it has to be said, is very real, as is their mutual dependence. Their relationship is symbiotic, each seeming to need the other to complete himself. The seriousness with which they take this has its comic aspects: Benn submits his experiences to Kenneth's judgement in order to understand them himself; Kenneth takes notes of their conversations so that he can analyse them. Even Benn's intimate sexual experiences come under this scrutiny, and he is certainly not reticent about describing them, making something of a voyeur out of Kenneth. So close is their attachment that when Benn marries into the Layamon family Kenneth thinks of himself as being carried into the family with his uncle, and when Benn talks about his prospective honeymoon Kenneth feels a twinge of jealousy, as if he has been 'cut out'. There are potential homoerotic implications here, of course, which Benn himself is at pains to deny when he rejects theoretical suspicion that men who marry beautiful women may be homosexual. Still, there is a sense that the two men have opted for weakness by allowing their relationship to protect them from the realities of the world, as is indicated by the story from Hoffmann that Kenneth alludes to at the end of the novel, a story which surely does suggest homosexuality. It may be that the love that both of them are seeking already exists between them.

As usual, Bellow obscures his own views by these narrative indirections. It should not be assumed, however, that the narrative indirections and the comic tone are intended to mitigate the pessimism suggested by Benn's retreat from the world. Kenneth's view, illustrated by the story he tells, is that 'historical forces are sending everybody straight to hell' (Ch. 2). His conviction that the Western world is in a state of cultural and intellectual crisis was certainly, in 1987, a conviction that Bellow himself held, as he demonstrated in his sympathetic foreword to Allan Bloom's highly controversial book *The Closing of the American Mind*, which appeared in that year.

In 1984 Bellow had published *Him with His Foot in His Mouth and Other Stories*, which included one long story, 'What Kind of Day Did You Have?', that is really a novella. It is interesting that, late in his career, Bellow should have found renewed interest in the short forms with which he began, for in 1989 he published two novellas, *A Theft* and *The Bellarosa Connection*. *A Theft* was published under rather odd circumstances. Bellow initially offered it for magazine publication, but the editors required that extensive cuts be made. Bellow was unwilling to agree to this, and instead had the book published in paperback form – a very unusual move for a writer of Bellow's stature. Although it is natural to sympathize with Bellow's insistence that his aesthetic judgement in the case was superior to that of the editors, it is not difficult to see why the editors wanted the cuts. The 'theft' of the novella's title does not actually take place until more than mid-way through, and the plot built around it is not very substantial and not always coherent. Presumably the magazine editors saw it as an over-extended short story, but it reads more like the skeleton of a much larger work. While it contains some energetic writing, there is almost no attempt to present the New York cityscape that is its setting, and while there are flashes of the kind of comic observation of character customary in Bellow's work, most of the characters are under-developed. Further, neither the intensity of feeling claimed for its central situation nor the nature of the self-knowledge that it reveals to the protagonist is clearly presented.

The critical response to the publication of *A Theft* was, as usual with Bellow's work, divided. While one reviewer was able to find enough of the novelist's characteristic humanity to call it 'vintage Bellow', many of those who read the novella in the context of his major work were disappointed, finding it 'on the thin side', or 'jumpy and skimpy'.[66] Even the most generous praise tended to be faint, like that of a reviewer in the *New York Review of Books*, who wrote that *A Theft* is 'a mildly pleasant read for admirers of Bellow, but it serves as a reminder of how much more we have come to expect of this writer'.[67] In a sense, however, it was precisely what readers had come to expect of Bellow that he challenged with *A Theft* by placing a woman at its centre. Some of his short stories, most notably 'What Kind of Day Did You Have?', have women as protagonists, but his refusal to allow *A Theft* to be a short story indicates that he saw it as having a special significance. He has said of the book, 'I do see *A Theft* as a departure. I suppose I am asking a reader to feel his way into regions never before visited'.[68] But these were regions Bellow himself had barely visited (only in the early short story 'Leaving the Yellow House' and the more recent 'What Kind of Day Did You Have?' is a woman at the centre), and to feel his way into them he had to present a psychology and to find a tone for its narrative presentation different from anything he had done before. It was, as the critical reception indicates, a risky venture.

As we have seen, Bellow has frequently been criticized for the difficulty he apparently found in creating women. In most of his early novels the women, whether wives or mistresses, are shadowy, often self-sacrificing figures kept on the margins of the story. Thea Fenchel in *The Adventures of Augie March* might be seen as the prototype of the characteristic Bellow woman: voluptuous and powerful, sensual and sexually liberated, educated in a dilettantish manner, with expensive, sophisticated tastes and making great demands of a man. She is the object of masculine desire who, when slighted, can become an emasculating terror: a Ramona, an Angela, a Renata can swiftly turn into a Madeleine or a Denise. Whatever her demands, her presence creates chaotic interference with the hero's intellectual work. In Bellow's previous novels, however, this alarming figure is always seen from the male perspective, through the distorting vision of a man who feels himself victimized. Bellow's new departure in *A Theft* was an attempt to make a woman the controlling consciousness of the narrative.

Clara Velde is an executive in a publishing company, dealing with matters of fashion. Now in her forties, she is married to her fourth husband, Wilder, by whom she has three daughters. The one real love of her life, however, is the high-flying Washington figure Ithiel Regler (she calls him 'Teddy'), with whom she has had a twenty-year affair, and who, in spite of her persuasion that they are the 'human pair' whose children would save the world, has managed over that time to avoid marrying her. Years before, Regler had given her an emerald ring which became for her the sentimental symbol of their love. The ring was once lost, and recovered long afterwards, though Clara did not return the insurance money that she had claimed for it. Now the ring has disappeared again, and she suspects that the Haitian boyfriend of her Austrian au pair Gina Wegman has stolen it. The simple plot tells of her efforts to retrieve the ring, efforts which illuminate and develop her relationships with Regler, Gina and her oldest daughter Lucy.

Clara shares much with the earlier female characters. She is handsome, sexy, with good legs, buys her clothes in the best shops, is full of 'personal force':

Really, everything about her was conspicuous, not only the size and shape of her head. She must have decided long ago that for the likes of her there could be no cover-up; she couldn't divert energy into disguises. So there she was, a rawboned American

woman. She had very good legs – who knows what you would
have seen if pioneer women had worn shorter skirts.   (Ch. 1)

It is possible to see from this passage from the book's opening
paragraph what difficulty Bellow had in presenting Clara. The
qualification in the second sentence ('She must have decided'
rather than 'She decided') implies an unwillingness fully to enter
her mind (the narrative voice is making an inference about
something it apparently doesn't know), and the emphasis on the
legs (those legs appear over and over again, almost an obsession, in
the narrative) reveals a masculine rather than a feminine gaze. It
may be that this difficulty of reproducing a feminine consciousness
is why so much of the book seems under-developed. The narrative
voice that here sees Clara from the outside does sometimes speak
from her perspective, but it generally takes an odd, chatty tone that
the author seems uncomfortable with. To get round this discom-
fort he allows Clara to tell much of her own story, to a Chinese-
American confidante named Laura Wong. Laura is an essentially
passive device, there to listen to Clara. When, near the end of the
novella, Clara decides that Laura wants to get Regler for herself,
the reader cannot understand it, because Laura is barely allowed to
exist as a character: 'She had been married too. Five years an
American wife. Maybe she had even been in love. She never said.
You'd never know' (Ch. 2).

Clara is the most fully-realized character in the book, but there is
much that we are not told even about her. The product of a
small-town, God-fearing Indiana upbringing, she was educated at
Bloomington, Wellesley, Cambridge and Columbia. She worked
for Reuters for a time, taught Classics, and wrote feature articles
for foreign newspapers before setting up her own journalistic
agency, which she sold to the international publishing company in
which she is now an executive. This is quite a career, and her life
has involved, as well as her four husbands, numerous lovers and
two suicide attempts. The problem is that although we are told all
of this, we see little of it. The world of fashion in which her great
abilities have made their mark is hardly described at all, being
represented by a suite of offices, a trade briefing on shoulder pads
and a show featuring such fashions as puffy knickers and simulated
beaver capes. It is ironic (and, no doubt, so intended) that a woman
presented as deep in feeling and thought should have built her
reputation out of expensive superficialities.

If the depiction of Clara is insubstantial, that of Ithiel Regler is much more so. Precisely what he does is never made clear. He is an expert on nuclear strategy, a magnetic television personality who interviews men like Anatoly Dobrynin, a political trouble-shooter who has the ear of Henry Kissinger and whose opinions are listened to by the Shah of Iran and the Venezuelan government. He has other large interests, though, helping a Japanese whiskey manufacturer to find a South American market and helping the Italian police to track down terrorists. He only does what he wants to do, however, and when he feels like a break he flies to the Olduvai Gorge to talk to Mr Leakey, presumably about anthropology. Clara herself has no doubts about his greatness; he is the standard against which all other men are judged, a man who more than any other understands the nature of the times. She thinks: 'Why, Ithiel could be the Gibbon or the Tacitus of the American Empire. ... If he wanted, he could do with Nixon, Johnson, Kennedy or Kissinger, with the Shah or de Gaulle, what Keynes had done with the Allies at Versailles' (Ch. 4). The improbability of all this does not seem to have escaped Bellow, as the name Ithiel Regler implies (a 'weird moniker', Regler calls it; the words suggest a meaning like 'angelic ruler').

The problem is to show the quality of such a world-class thinker. Bellow had attempted something of the sort with Herzog, Mr Sammler and Benn Crader. But Regler comes out with ideas like this: 'Neither the Russians nor the Americans can manage the world. Not capable of organising the future'. And Clara is so impressed by it that she thinks of setting up a fund so that Regler can publish his thoughts. Later, when she is trying to find Gina, who has left home after the theft of the ring, she goes to Ithiel for advice and he suggests that she hire a private investigator. Her response is to say to him, 'I can see why General Haig and such people call on you to analyze the Iranians or the Russians' (Ch. 5). This response might have been mock-naive, for Clara 'recognized the comic appeal of being the openmouthed rube' (Ch. 2). But there is no indication here that she does not mean her praise seriously, and the effect is of preposterous inflation.

The relationship between these two, at least from Clara's point of view, is symbolized by the ring. The ring comes to signify not just the love that she shares with Regler, but 'love' on a more general scale. When she loses it, the effect on her feelings is profound, though it hardly seems to worry Regler at all. The loss also affects her relationship with Gina, for whom she has conceived a maternal affection. She sees Gina as an innocent who must be protected from the potentially crushing energies of New York (she constantly refers to the city as 'Gogmagogsville', suggesting that its Satanic forces have brought it close to Armageddon). The trust that has developed between them is violated by the theft of the ring by Gina's Haitian boyfriend, and the fact that it was removed from her bedroom, her inner sanctum, seems to Clara to augment her sense of having been violated. The theft lets in the terrible predatory forces of Gogmagogsville, forces that deny love. Consequently, the effort that Gina makes to retrieve the ring becomes a sign of hope for Clara.

Because we see so little of Gina, because her character is so lightly sketched, we do not see why Clara has become so fond of her. The important revelatory function she performs at the end of the story is, consequently, difficult to accept. Clara meets her at the Westbury Hotel to discuss the circumstances of the return of the ring. She discovers that this restoration involved an act of enterprise and maturity by her daughter Lucy. Lucy is a clumsy, persecuted girl whose vulnerability has contributed much to Clara's fears for the future, but Gina shows how much of Clara's strength Lucy has in her. She also points Clara towards a new self-understanding: 'With all the disorder, I can't see how you keep track. You do, though. I believe you pretty well know who you are' (Ch. 6). The novella ends with a burst of cathartic emotion:

> The main source of tears came open. She found a handkerchief and held it to her face in her ringed hand, striding in an awkward hurry. She might have been treading water in New York harbour – it felt that way, more a sea than a pavement, and for all the effort and the motions that she made, she wasn't getting anywhere, she was still in the same place.   (Ch. 6)

This scene of weeping and drowning is reminiscent of the ending of *Seize the Day*, but whereas the source of Tommy Wilhelm's tears was a pity for himself and for mankind, Clara's emotion is affirmative: 'I do seem to have an idea who it is that's at the middle of me. There may not be more than one in a xillion, more's the pity, that do have. And my own child possibly one of those' (Ch. 6).

A Theft implies much more than it says. We are told of a culture in decline, but the distressed American cityscape that Bellow created so vividly in earlier novels is never shown to us. Instead, the horrors of Gogmagogsville are embodied in the Haitian thief Frederic, who is treated by the narrative with no little contempt – we are a long way from the 'noble' black criminal of *Mr Sammler's Planet*. The threat to civilization becomes, rather, the threat of Harlem to Park Avenue, and it is difficult to see the pampered fashion consultant with her suite of offices and her livery service as the representative of anything that really matters. Indeed, Clara hardly has the right to resent Frederic's theft of the ring, since she was guilty of a theft of equivalent magnitude when she failed to return the insurance money. The larger meanings attached to the ring, about the need for love in the world, simply to not show themselves with any clarity.

Where the novella shows real vitality is on its margins. While the tone of the treatment of Clara and Regler is insecure, there is a sureness of touch in the comic treatment of minor characters: Clara's feckless, complacent husband Wilder, dumb enough to be a congressman; the ludicrous billionaire Giangiacomo arguing the need for revolutionary action while his butler serves truffles; Clara's psychiatrist Dr Gladstone, with his 'samurai beard, the bared teeth it framed, the big fashionable specs' (Ch. 5), convinced that her dependence on the ring is a dependence on him because the ring has a precious stone in it and he has 'stone' in his name. All these are presented with comic precision, and we wish for more of them in a book that, for all its brevity, is loose, unfocused, and lacking the intensity and compression to be found in Bellow's earlier novellas.

With his second novella of 1989, *The Bellarosa Connection*, Bellow returned to more characteristic preoccupations: the fate of the Jewish people, the future of America, the uses of memory, the value of a life. The 'connection' of the title refers to an organization supposedly operated by the Broadway showman Billy Rose to smuggle Jews out of wartime Italy. One of those he aided was Harry Fonstein, who escaped via Cuba (where he met his 'tiger wife', the fat, formidable Sorella) to America, and built a successful business. Driven by a desire to thank his benefactor in person Fonstein spent some years trying to arrange a meeting with Rose, but was always rebuffed, and finally gave up. Sorella, however, believed that that part of Fonstein's life could never be completed unless he met Rose. Near the end of the fifties she arranged a visit to Jerusalem, knowing that Rose was going there to donate a

sculpture garden. Armed with a dossier documenting Rose's shady
business and sexual affairs, she confronted him in the King David
Hotel, hoping to force him to receive Fonstein. What she found,
however, was a contemptible, sleazy figure who had no interest in
the lives of those he had aided, and in disgust she left him alone.

This history is recounted to us in the immediate present by a
narrator who remains unnamed throughout, though we learn
much about him. Born in New Jersey of a Russian Jewish family, he
turned his extraordinary powers of memory into a business and
built a fortune as founder of the Mnemosyne Institute, in which he
trained others in the use of memory. He married a woman of old
Anglo-Saxon Protestant stock and now, in his seventies, widowed
and retired, he lives alone in a great Philadelphia mansion. His life
intersected twice with that of the Fonsteins. He first met them some
forty years earlier, when Harry, the nephew of his stepmother, had
just arrived from Cuba. He did not see them again for more than
ten years, and then he met them by chance in the lobby of the King
David Hotel. This encounter in Jerusalem was the last time he saw
them, and the history he gives us derives entirely from these two
periods, since the only subsequent contact he had with them was a
telephone call from Harry to discuss the education of their son
Gilbert, a prodigy in mathematics. At the time of his narrative,
however, his interest in the Fonsteins has been revived by a request
for help in locating them. His attempts to find them necessitate
contacting long-neglected (and resentful) acquaintances, and he
finally discovers that they died in a road accident six months earlier
as they were driving to Atlantic City to aid their son who had got
into trouble through gambling.

The main interest in this story derives from the way in which the
narrator reconstitutes its incidents through an act of memory, and
begins to see a new significance in them: that the Fonsteins, who
had long seemed interesting but marginal to him, might have
contributed something important to his experience, and that the
meaning of the Fonsteins' lives has much to do with the meaning of
his own. His narration has a dual perspective, because his accurate
memory allows him to recall events from the past exactly as he had
originally perceived them, while he is now able to see the inadequacy of that perception, and gropes for a better understanding.
Fundamental to this reconstruction is a question raised by Sorella
when she tries to explain Rose's behaviour: 'The Jews could survive
everything that Europe threw at them. I mean the lucky remnant.

But now comes the next test – America. Can they hold their ground, or will the U.S.A. be too much for them?' (Ch. 2).

Rose's actions in the story remain something of a puzzle. The real-life Billy Rose was a song-writer and impresario, a night-club owner, a producer of Broadway spectacles of immense vulgarity. He was, that is, associated with the kind of escapist vision of life represented in the novella by Broadway, Hollywood and Las Vegas. Thus the fictional scheme for rescuing Jews from Fascist Europe is directly associated with such fantasy: 'He must've seen Leslie Howard in *The Scarlet Pimpernel*' (Ch. 1), the narrator suggests, and even the romantic sound of the conversion of Rose's misheard name to 'Bellarosa' holds something of this. Although his actions were prompted by deep (if vestigial) feelings of Jewishness, he was not capable of understanding the experience of the European Jews. Sorella presents a truer perspective when she says of the crippled adolescent Fonstein struggling through Italy 'He couldn't vault over walls like Douglas Fairbanks' (Ch. 1). Rose's theatrical constructions (we should note that he himself is a theatrical construction, unable to function in Jerusalem without his costume, the expensive clothing that allows him to play the part of the 'Broadway personage') are a means of evading reality, like the 'Hollywood style' extravaganza he made out of the American Jews' statement against the War Against the Jews.

And yet the story of Billy Rose is a great American success story: the poor Jew with cunning and enterprise who knew that in America you can sell anything and who made it big by selling escape. But the kind of escape from reality that he had been selling to the American masses made it impossible for him to understand the reality of the escape that he had made possible for Fonstein. This is what Sorella is referring to when she asks whether the U.S.A. will be too much for the Jews: will it cut them off from an understanding of the special experience of their race? When Sorella confronts Rose and demands that he remember her husband Rose asks 'Remember, forget – what's the difference to me?' (Ch. 1). But Sorella knows that Fonstein's experience was a Jewish experience, 'a part of the destruction of the Jews' (Ch. 1), and not to remember it is to deny it. When the narrator meets the Fonsteins in Jerusalem he is aware that Harry is still the man who has suffered, and that his memory is constantly at work on the past. In the contrast between Rose and Fonstein lies part of the answer to Sorella's question.

What America does to the Jew, the novella implies, is to make him forget what it means to be a Jew, to make him forget the suffering that has been the Jewish fate. This theme is explored not so much through the contrast between Fonstein and Rose as through that between Fonstein and the narrator, for one of the alarming discoveries the narrator makes when he reconstructs the Fonsteins' story is that he is closer to Rose than to Fonstein: 'I was a Jew of an entirely different breed. And therefore (yes, go on, you can't avoid it now) closer to Billy Rose and his rescue operation, the personal underground inspired by *The Scarlet Pimpernel* – the Hollywood of Leslie Howard who acted the Pimpernel. ... You pay a price for being a child of the New World' (Ch. 2). The price he has to pay, communicated to him through a dream, is the discovery that he has never really understood the kind of merciless brutality that is the Jewish experience, such as is emblematically represented in the figure of the old madman in Jerusalem who sets him off on his search for the Fonsteins, 'abused out of his head by persecution, loss, death, and brutal history' (Ch. 2).

The story implies that this failure of the Americanized Jews arises from a conscious act of the will, and it is here that the narrator's concern with memory becomes important. Billy Rose's refusal to acknowledge Fonstein is a denial of a part of his own history, and the narrator himself is guilty of a similar denial. His worldly success has its foundation on his own discovery of the commercial potential of memory. This made him a fortune and allowed him to marry a Wasp lady and become a Philadelphian; it also estranged him from his father and his cultural origins, represented by his upbringing in New Jersey: 'Whenever possible I omitted New Jersey' (Ch. 1), he says, meaning that by an act of will, a denial of memory, he effaced his Jewish roots. His secession from his own history is reflected in his present isolation in his Wasp mansion, but its seeds were there in the past, at the time of his first encounters with Fonstein. Fonstein's sufferings gave him a weight and seriousness that the dilettantish narrator lacked; the latter's self-conscious cleverness is nicely caught in his own description of the contrast: 'Surviving-Fonstein, with all the furies of Europe at his back, made me look bad' (Ch. 1). The callow wit of the statement manages to acknowledge Fonstein's suffering without in any way understanding it.

The character who does understand Fonstein's suffering is his wife Sorella, the moral centre of the story. Sorella is an extraordinary creation; the comic treatment of her extreme fatness in no way undermines the dignity and seriousness of what she represents. Indeed, the comic treatment is necessary, for it is through transcending the rejection and humiliation that her immensity brought upon her in the past that Sorella was able to achieve imaginative identification with Fonstein's experience and an awareness of the crucial importance of maintaining its memory. Her climactic recognition that Billy Rose is not fit to associate with her husband is in one sense a triumph, a demonstration of her own superiority, but it is also an admission of her defeat by American spiritual vacuity. As a defeat it was prefigured by the narrator, who in response to her attempts to get him to think about the Holocaust refused her challenge: 'I didn't want to think of the history and psychology of these abominations, death chambers and furnaces' (Ch. 1). It is followed by a rather more terribly ironic defeat.

The Fonsteins' son Gilbert is a mathematical prodigy for whom Sorella has great hopes. Summing up her confrontation with Rose she says 'from start to finish it was a one-hundred-percent American event, of our own generation. It'll be different for our children' (Ch. 1). But it is not different for Gilbert, who finds a way of selling his abilities, and uses his mathematical genius for developing systems to win at gambling. On a literal level this destroys his parents, for they are killed in a car crash while on their way to Atlantic City to extricate him from trouble that he has got into through his gambling. On a metaphorical level the destruction is greater, for at the end of the novella we are told that he has little interest in being a Jew, and that he is in Las Vegas, 'the heart of the American entertainment industry', operating a gambling system that involves memorizing cards. His career, that is, recapitulates the careers of Billy Rose and the narrator himself, combines show-biz with memory, and implies the inevitability of the corruption of the Americanized Jew. This would seem to be a highly pessimistic conclusion to the novella.

The ending of *The Bellarosa Connection*, like all Bellow's endings, allows for conflicting responses. This led some reviewers to claim that the ending does not tie things together, or that it is a conclusion in which nothing is concluded.[69] But perhaps something may be concluded. The final sentence has the narrator recording everything he can remember about the Bellarosa Connection 'with a Mnemosyne flourish'. The whole novel, that is, is presented as an act of memory. What does this mean? 'Memory is life', the novella keeps saying, but also, 'memory is a curse', Billy Rose sees only the second of these truths, so he refuses to remember. The narrator, more sophisticated in the ways of memory, must find more complex ways to deal with the curse. In a sense, he reverses the proposition: life is memory; or, perhaps more accurately, a life is a memorial reconstruction. In recording everything he can remember of the Bellarosa Connection, in reconstructing the Fonsteins' lives, he appears to be trying to reconstruct his own and to incorporate their real experience in it. Fonstein's suffering is a part of Jewish history and it must be recognized. This is what Sorella's life means, for it has been dedicated to bringing about that recognition. The narrator's growing apprehension of Sorella's ethical significance, his need of the heroic feminine sensibility, along with his recognition of his failure to understand the Jewish experience of brutality, open up the possibility of a healing awareness. In telling the story he is also learning from it and relocating himself inside Jewish history. Having long desired isolation, he finally finds himself 'with an acute need for conversation' (Ch. 2).

   The mood of *The Bellarosa Connection* is elegiac, deeply concerned with what is lost. This is very much a book about old age. At one point the narrator is shaken because he cannot remember the word 'Swanee' in a song that he has known for 70 years: for him, loss of memory is loss of life. At another point, like the aged scarecrow-man in Yeats's poem 'Sailing to Byzantium', he is impatient with his own physical degeneration: 'One does grow weary of taking care of this man-sized doll, the elderly retiree, giving him his pills, pulling on his socks, spooning up his cornflakes, shaving his face, seeing to it that he gets his sleep' (Ch. 2). His soul is just a sitter in his body. Yet, like Yeats's old man, Bellow's literary soul claps its hands and sings louder, for this book, despite its concern with deterioration, is full of energy and wit, a fine addition to the Bellow canon.

6

Short Stories

Although Bellow began his career with the small-scale works *Dangling Man* and *The Victim*, he is best known for substantial novels like *The Adventures of Augie March* and *Herzog*, and it is generally accepted that his talents are best represented in these sprawling forms. He has, however, contributed excellent short stories to periodicals as diverse as *Partisan Review* and *Playboy*. Some at least of these stories he felt deserved a wider audience, and they have been reprinted in two collections, *Mosby's Memoirs and Other Stories* (1968), and *Him with His Foot in His Mouth and Other Stories* (1984).

Mosby's Memoirs brings together six stories written over a period of about seventeen years, including the three that were published with *Seize the Day*. Each of these three concerns in some way an attempt by an individual to establish for himself an identity in relation to the outside world which will allow inner and outer realities to give stable meaning to each other. The earliest, 'Looking for Mr. Green' (1951), set in the bleak Chicago of the depression years, concerns the attempts of George Grebe, a displaced academic, to deliver a welfare cheque to a Mr Green. During his journey through the black slum district he is met with suspicion and denials that make him ponder the insubstantiality of identity, and this leads him to question the possibility of establishing the existence of a stable reality. The misery and dismal ugliness of this world are one sort of reality, a product of human history and human consent, and he cannot bring himself to believe that there is not a higher reality beyond it. His quest to find Mr Green becomes in his mind a quest for this higher reality, but when he finally finds Green's house he is confronted by a drunken, naked woman. Her refusal to either confirm or deny the presence of Mr Green or that she is Mrs Green appears to discredit his idea of a higher reality, but he gives her the cheque, convincing himself that Mr Green *is* there, and can be found.

119

The protagonist of 'The Gonzaga Manuscripts' (1954) also undertakes an unsuccessful quest, but unlike Grebe he is unable to allow himself the consolation of a conviction that what he seeks is, somehow, there. Clarence Feiler has gone to Spain to try to locate manuscripts of poems by a dead Spanish writer whom he admires for his positive acceptance of the world as it is and of his place as a 'creature' in it. The existence of the Gonzaga manuscripts matters to him much as the existence of Mr Green matters to Grebe. The people he meets in his search are not interested in Gonzaga, however, and show nothing of the Gonzagian spirit that Feiler so values, being more concerned with the weaknesses of Gonzaga's flesh, and assuming that Feiler's own concerns with the poet must be materialistic. Benumbed by his experience, he has to abandon not only his quest but also the vision of human possibility that it has held out for him.

The material burden of the world weighs heavily on Rogin, the protagonist of 'A Father-to-Be' (1955), in a different way. He is oppressed by his financial commitments to his brother and his mother, and, most of all, by the lavish spending of Joan, his fiancée, who is beautiful, educated and refined, but unable to find 'suitable' employment. On his way to supper at her home one evening he sees on the subway a middle-aged man who is remarkably like Joan in appearance, and imagines that this is what their son will look like in 40 years' time. But the man is all that Rogin despises: fourth-rate, ordinary, dull, self-satisfied and fundamentally bourgeois; and Rogin becomes enraged at the injustice of this, the fact that his personal aims should count for nothing in the creation of the future, and also resentful at Joan for this further pressure he thinks she has imposed on him. When he arrives at her house, however, she persuades him to let her wash his hair, and overwhelmed by her female tenderness he abandons his determination to assert himself. Like the other two stories, 'A Father-to-Be' is concerned in part with the crushing weight of the material on the human spirit. In all of them money is the source of the denial of this higher humanity: Grebe tries to hold on to a vision of something ulterior to the physical reality that money has created; Feiler's idealism is inextricably bound up with an idea of artistic value that is exploded by his discovery of the acquisitive and destructive interests of those he confronts; Rogin, worried about his own financial troubles, takes ironic comfort from the idea that all are oppressed and afflicted.

'Leaving the Yellow House' was first published in 1957, while Bellow was working on *Henderson the Rain King*. It is the story of Hattie Waggoner, an old woman living alone in an isolated house in the Utah Desert. Faced with her own declining powers and approaching death, Hattie decides to make her will. The only thing she has to bequeath is her house which is, in a sense, her identity; she loves it, and yet it imprisons her, and its isolation is a metaphor for her own. As she considers the possible recipients of her bequest she goes back in memory over her life, finding there loss and defeat, and realizes that her only intimacy is with herself, and so in a gesture of defiance against a world that hasn't given her much she leaves her house to herself. Hattie is a large, cheerfully comic woman, both drunkenly self-destructive and resilient (she has much in common with Henderson). She combines snobbish pride in her Philadelphia family with a desire to show herself tough enough to flourish in the Western cowboy country, but the result is that she is an alien in the land she inhabits. Her gesture does nothing to save her, nothing to relieve the barrenness of her existence, but it is an act of persistence; like many Bellow heroes, she insists on survival against all odds. This is a good story, and it shows Bellow experimenting with a number of things. He tentatively employs the dual third person/first person narrative that he develops fully in *Herzog*, and he begins to explore the functions of memory (Hattie is made into a kind of spectator of her own life, watching it as if it were a film). Perhaps most notably, he creates his first female protagonist; and since she is not seen from a misogynist male perspective, like so many of Bellow's women, she is totally believable.

'The Old System' (1967) is more completely a story of memory. Dr Samuel Braun is a biochemist whose work involves the chemistry of heredity, the science of biological connectedness and continuity. As a scientist he wants to look at life with a cold eye, to fit things into rational systems, but his story is concerned with the disordered vitality of human emotion. It begins with his love for his cousin Isaac, now dead. Isaac had offended his sister Tina over a matter of money; he was not at fault, but his sister's irrational resentment caused a rift between them that Isaac tried often to repair, but it was healed only on Tina's deathbed. Dr Braun tries to understand this 'crude circus of feelings', and to do so he excavates his memory, tracing his family's American history to its pre-history in Russia. The story he digs up ends with a reconciliation, which he sees as a reassertion of the 'old laws and wisdom', the old Jewish system of blood ties, of obligation and acceptance, but his own scientific system remains inadequate as a means of understanding the demands of emotional life. 'The Old System' appeared while Bellow was working on *Mr. Sammler's Planet*, and it shares some of the novel's concerns; the aging Dr Braun, lying on his December bed, considering problems of memory, meaning and mortality, foreshadows the more complex Mr Sammler. It also takes up an issue that Bellow was later to pursue more fully in *The Dean's December* and *More Die of Heartbreak*: the ability of scientific thought to give order and meaning to human existence.

'Mosby's Memoirs' (1968) is the most complex of the six narratives. Willis Mosby is a retired academic and diplomat who is in Mexico writing his memoirs. He looks back with no small vanity on his successful career as confidant and advisor to distinguished men, a career founded on his intellectual arrogance and aggressiveness. In order to avoid what he calls 'the common fate of intellectuals', the sin of pride (he is unaware of how deeply guilty he is of this sin), he decides to temper the serious stuff of his autobiography by introducing into it, as comic relief, the story of a Jewish radical named Lustgarten whom he had met in post-war Paris. Lustgarten was a born loser, a naive, well-meaning figure who failed in everything he did, a man doomed to be victimized by life. Mosby considers this man with detached irony and no compassion, seeing him purely as a comic figure. Only at the end of the story do we learn what Mosby has almost suppressed – that by making Lustgarten appear comic to his own wife as a means of seducing her, he had participated in Lustgarten's victimization. This memory triggers a wave of guilt in Mosby, expressed in a feeling of suffocation, as if he is being crushed by the realization that his stance of intellectual superiority has drained him of all humanity. Bellow provides us here with a further sophistication of the technique of moving in and out of the third-person narrative voice. Like the historian Henry Adams, with whom he compares himself favourably but inappropriately, Mosby thinks of himself in the third person. This is an attempt (like Dr Braun's) to see life objectively, but also, as it turns out, to distance himself from what he does not wish to confront: his own coldness and isolation. For all his intellectual acumen (and, as presented in the story, that is very real) Mosby has been blind to the deeper truths of his existence, and is doomed to live out his life being what he is.

The earliest of the five stories collected in *Him with His Foot in His Mouth* is 'Zetland: By a Character Witness' (1974). This is hardly a story at all; it is a character sketch extracted from material developed for *Humboldt's Gift*, a memoir of the doomed poet Isaac Rosenfeld. It is an affectionate portrait of the son of a Russian immigrant family (not unlike Bellow's own). It follows him from his bookish boyhood in Chicago, where he becomes a student of philosophy, to his life in New York where, after reading *Moby Dick*, he decides he has to give up philosophy, moves to Greenwich Village and takes up a bohemian life-style, immersed in experimental literature and radical politics. Fragmentary though the story is, it builds the life of Zetland out of the piled-up detail of a rich world. If Bellow had developed the story, he would probably have clarified the character of the narrator, the character witness who retrieves Zetland from his own memory, perhaps as a kind of mirror to his own life.

In most of Bellow's novels the protagonist's relationship with his father, if it exists at all, is a marginal part of the story, and is always uneasy and fractured, a source of pain in his memory, as it is for Henderson and Herzog; only in *Seize the Day* is it at the centre of the story. Like *Seize the Day*, 'A Silver Dish' (1978) is the story of a man whose life is blighted by his need to be loved by a father who is incapable of giving love. Woody Selbst is a successful businessman in his sixties who attempts to come to an understanding of his relationship with his recently-deceased father. The cynically selfish Morris Selbst had abandoned his family while Woody was still a child, but had always been able to cajole money out of his son. Woody's memory fixes on an incident that had taken place 40 years earlier, when his father had persuaded him to ask for money from the wealthy widow who was paying for Woody's education at a seminary. Woody had reluctantly agreed, though he suspected (rightly) that his father wanted the money for gambling; Morris repaid the woman's generosity by stealing a silver tray from her.

Woody tries to understand his father's action in terms of a kind of noble manhood, a refusal to accept the hypocrisy and feminine religiosity of the respectable seminary world. He needs to believe that, in some way, his father loved him, and that he himself shares some of that manhood (he likes to live slightly outside the law as a proof of this), but in fact his father was incapable of loving anyone, and, indeed, frequently chided Woody for not being selfish enough. Woody is actually quite unlike his father, having visions of a world of love and being fully aware of his obligations to others (he supports his mother and sister, his wife, and his mistress all in different households). The story links two moments of physical struggle: Woody had grappled with his father in an attempt to make him return the silver dish but was unsuccessful; 40 years later he had grappled with him on his deathbed to prevent him from removing the tubes and needles that were keeping him alive, but Morris defeated him once again and died in his arms. Woody's real struggle, however, is with himself (the hint in the name 'Selbst' – German for 'self' – is perhaps a little too obvious) as he attempts to forge that impossible link: for his own emotional and spiritual equilibrium he needs to redeem a man who cannot be redeemed.

'Him with His Foot in His Mouth' (1982) also begins with an act of memory that instigates a self-examination. Shawmut, the narrator, is an aging intellectual, a musicologist and TV guru who is living in exile in British Columbia, waiting to be extradited because of his involvement in shady financial affairs. A letter from an old friend reminds him of an incident that took place 35 years before. Shawmut gratuitously insulted a librarian at the college where he was teaching and this, he is told, wounded her for life. The story is Shawmut's letter of apology to the woman, but it becomes a survey of his life and of the character traits that have led him to this exile. His insult was only one of a series of similar incidents, which he attributes to a kind of uncontrollable reflex of wit (what he calls a *fatum*). What he reveals about himself, however, is a general ineptitude at life, and especially a failure with American materialism, that has allowed him to be swindled by his loved brother and to care for his aged mother who doesn't recognize him even though she remembers all her other children. His sense of his own value and cleverness is thus weighed against a character that has brought him to spiritual barrenness and his isolation in an alien land, and the reader's response falls between sympathy for Shawmut's loneliness and an ironic awareness of his culpability.

In each of these stories the protagonist's recollection of the past leads to a re-shaping of his life and a revelation to the reader of things that the protagonist himself does not clearly understand. 'Cousins' (1984) presents another, more complex account of an attempt, through memory, to reconcile past and present. Ijah Brodsky, the narrator, is an expert in law, like Shawmut an ideas-man turned television celebrity. He is asked to intercede with a judge on behalf of his cousin Tanky, and agrees to do so because of past ties (he calls his cousins 'the elect of my memory'). This gets him involved in the affairs of a number of other cousins. Ijah wants to feel that he is loved and admired by his cousins, though it appears that most of them, materialists that they are, have a degree of contempt for him, and are merely using him. One cousin, Scholem, is in genuine need of Ijah's help. Scholem is the other intellectual of the family; as a youth he was a philosopher with ground-breaking ideas, and made Ijah feel inferior. He is now a taxi-driver, and seeks Ijah's help with publication of his papers, and also with securing permission to be buried in East Germany.

For all his keen intelligence, Ijah has problems. He appears to have allowed his cousins to take the place of any closer family ties (he says nothing about his parents or siblings), and this may have been a stratagem for distancing people rather than connecting to them, for in spite of his professed love for his cousins he has seen them quite rarely; his cousin Mendy, for example, he contacts for the first time in decades, though he claims to have 'friendly and even affectionate relations' with him. He seems to have problems with closer relationships; he divorced his wife years before, and she subsequently had other husbands, but Ijah still thinks vaguely that she wants him – another example of his need of the esteem of others. The one real love of his life, a concert harpist called Virgie Dunton whom he has met perhaps five times in thirty years, is unattainable and therefore safe. Perhaps his real state of being is represented in the darkness of his apartment with its strange, oriental corners, and in his interest in Arctic exploration. His eagerness to believe in cousinly ties as representing love in the world (he thinks of the books of his schooldays with titles like 'Our Little Russian Cousins') coexists with the dark and cold of essential isolation. His final meeting with Scholem, when he suddenly realizes that he has been mistaken in his memories and his assessment of this cousin, comes as a kind of epiphany, a sudden re-assessment of himself.

The remaining story, 'What Kind of Day Did You Have?' is of interest first of all because it has in Katrina Goliger Bellow's second female protagonist. Katrina is a middle-aged woman who lives in a Chicago suburb; she is going through the messy fall-out of a divorce that became necessary because of her affair with Victor Wulpy, 'a world-class intellectual, big in the art world,' now in his seventies. The story covers a period of 24 hours, beginning as she is having dinner with her admirer, Sam Krieggstein, who claims to be a police lieutenant. Victor, who is giving a lecture in Buffalo, calls her to meet him there and then return with him to Chicago, and although this causes her much inconvenience with her psychiatrist, her children and her housekeeper, she agrees to join him. It is a stormy day, and on the return journey they are marooned in the airport in Detroit. With growing anxiety she realizes that she will not be able to get back to Chicago before her daughters return home from school, and since she has had to lie about her trip, she fears that this will give ammunition to her vengeful ex-husband. Her fears seem to be justified when she finally gets back home and finds the house empty, and she rushes out in panic, to discover that Krieggstein has taken care of the children. She ends her day on the verge of emotional collapse.

As this outline indicates, Katrina is something of a victim. She is an intelligent woman, but she has little self-esteem. She was mocked in childhood by a father who called her 'Dumb Dora', and her marriage to a social climber who needed her only as a housewife gave her little opportunity to develop herself. Her envious sister Dorothea claims that Katrina has nothing to offer the intellectual high-flier but her body. Katrina half believes this, and in order to achieve some measure of independence and a sense of her own value she has been trying to write a story for children about an elephant trapped in a department store, but cannot find a way of ending it, which gives her a frustrating sense of failure. To be needed by Victor, therefore, allows her some sense of worth.

'How do you assess a woman who knows how to bind such a wizard to her?' the narrative voice asks, and the problem of this story seems to be that Katrina is valued not for anything intrinsic in her, but as she is perceived by Victor. Victor is viewed by that same narrative voice with no little admiration; words like 'wizard' and 'giant' appear frequently. At parties, the only voice to be heard is Victor's, as he monopolizes all conversations; his opinions are sought at the highest levels of political and economic activity. To the reader, however, he may appear overbearingly arrogant. He gives a talk at a university, but perceives no signs of intelligence in his audience; pursued by an old acquaintance, a successful film-maker who craves a good conversation about ideas, he is rude and hostile. Katrina herself remembers with pain how she was once the recipient of his long-lasting contempt when she persuaded him to go with her to see the film *MASH*.

Katrina craves distinction, and she believes she is getting it by having Victor confide his thoughts in her: 'Abed, Victor and Katrina smoked, drank . . . they *thought* – my God, they thought'. But it is Victor's thinking that counts, because he doesn't listen to the thoughts of others. Indeed, he has little interest in Katrina's mind, let alone respect for it: 'She could irritate him to the point of heartbreak'. He has erotic fantasies about her, she keeps him going, and this inexplicable sexual chemistry is the source of his tie to her. For all his genius, he is incapable of understanding a life different from his own, and her desire to have him say he loves her is meaningless to him; he can only respond to it with contempt. His need, perhaps, is summed up in the Picasso engravings described in the story, voyeuristic depictions of old men, satyr-artists gazing at submissive female bodies ('wide-open odalisques').

Katrina wants to grow, to break out of the self defined by her father and her husband, and Victor's demanding intellectual company seems to be a way for her to do that. But the assumption of her inferiority by both Victor and herself means that she remains in the trap. She is like the elephant in her story, and is no more capable of extricating herself than she is of freeing the elephant. 'What Kind of Day Did You Have?' has much sympathy for Katrina, yet we can't help feeling, as we read, that Bellow's real interest is with Victor Wulpy.

'What Kind of Day Did You Have' is much more substantial than the other stories in this collection; it is really a novella. It is as long as *Seize the Day*, as long as the later work *A Theft*, with which it has much in common. Bellow, late in his career, seems to have turned away from the sprawling novels that are generally taken to be his forte to the cleaner lines of these shorter forms. The central issues of his larger novels are still here, but the extended presentation of ideas in the novels from *Herzog* onwards is not possible, and there is less room for the didacticism, the lecturing that for many readers mars his major work.

7

Literary Status

There seems little reason to doubt that Bellow will remain a significant figure in the landscape of twentieth-century American literature: the range and seriousness of the body of work he has produced will ensure that. The accumulation of scholarly analysis of his writing is immense, and there is even a journal dedicated solely to his work, but it would be a pity if he were to be nothing more than grist for the academic mill. He does, however, seem to have evaded the fate of many serious novelists who have been unable to generate a popular following, for his novels usually reach the top ten of the best-seller lists. While it is easy to predict his continuing prominence within the American literary tradition, it is less easy to say precisely where he stands in it.

The prevailing fictional direction when Bellow began writing was the modernist, and he attempted to distance himself from this (at least as it was currently represented by such writers as Hemingway) in the opening words of his first novel. *Dangling Man* showed a clear indebtedness to European influences, as did *The Victim*, and critics read his early work in the light of European existentialism, seeing his dangling men as alienated figures vainly trying to puzzle out the meaning of 'reality': as Irving Malin notes in the introduction to his 1967 collection of essays on Bellow, the theme of alienation is emphasized by all twelve of the critics who contributed to it.[70] But this reading of Bellow was complicated with the publication of *The Adventures of Augie March*, which showed a new set of influences. The title, with its clear echo of Twain's *The Adventures of Huckleberry Finn*, proclaimed the novel an *American* novel, as did the modification of the voice of Walt Whitman, and the wonderful evocation of material solidity and urban energies that linked it with the Naturalism of such earlier Chicago writers as Theodore Dreiser. In this novel and those that followed it Bellow developed with increasing confidence a voice that combined the intellectual subtlety and range of his European models with a demotic American raciness, a voice that many critics have found distinctive enough to merit the coinage 'Bellovian'.

Bellow's great distinction is to have adapted and contained the influences that have worked upon him, so that he cannot be said to stand directly in a line with any of them. According to Harold Bloom, employing a metaphor derived from the Freudian observation of the son's compulsion to engage with and destroy the father, strong writers need to preserve or assert their identity through a struggle to 'defeat' the strong writers of the previous generation.[71] In only one of his novels, *Humboldt's Gift*, does Bellow concern himself directly with a writer's relationship with a literary 'father'. In many of them, however, the hero's relationship with his father is troubled or even severed. Herzog, probing his past, finds himself probing the wound of a deeply fractured relationship with his father; so does Henderson. Augie March, who has never known his own father, is able to construct an image of the absent father to suit his needs in the creation of his identity. Perhaps Bellow is like Augie. It may be that his own ambivalence about this 'anxiety of influence' makes him construct himself as a writer out of such a range of sources, denying any real 'father'. After all, Tommy Wilhelm's experience suggests that the father can never really be defeated.

Certainly, when critics have attempted to associate Bellow with a 'tradition' or 'school' of writing, he has taken some pains to discredit the association. This is particularly true of the inevitable designation of him as a Jewish-American novelist. There is a line of Jewish immigrant novels leading back to Abraham Cahan's *The Rise of David Levinsky* (1917); the thirties saw the production of Daniel Fuchs' books about New York slum life, of Henry Roth's single, brilliant novel, *Call It Sleep*, and of the horrified satirical fictions of Nathaniel West. When in the early fifties Bellow associated himself with the *Partisan Review* circle, he met writers like Delmore Schwartz. With the appearance around that time of a new generation of Jewish novelists, most notably Bernard Malamud and Philip Roth, it is not surprising that critics should have perceived a major 'movement' that would lead fiction on from modernism, with Bellow as a prominent figure in it. Bellow resisted this definition, however; when he received the Nobel Prize he designated himself 'an American writer and a Jew', and was criticized for his faulty priority, but he has made clear why he takes this attitude: 'I am a

Jew, and I have written some books. I have tried to fit my soul into the Jewish-writer category, but it does not feel comfortably accommodated there'.[72] The problem, for Bellow, is one of the constraint or limitation imposed on a writer who is categorized in this way.

Still, although Bellow may resist fitting his soul into the Jewish-writer category, the fact that he is Jewish has been of undeniable importance both for the material of his fiction and for his stance as a writer. The sense of displacement that lies at the centre of Bellow's Jewish immigrant experience is what generates in him the larger sense of being an outsider set in an adversary relationship with the society he has to inhabit. It is fundamental to the experience of each of Bellow's protagonists, and this is as true of the Gentile Henderson and Corde as it is of the others. The Bellow hero thus shares the author's sense of an obligation to maintain a constant critical scrutiny of the values of the society he inhabits. Bellow himself finds his values in a broad and deep spiritual and intellectual culture, and upon this some at least of his characters are able to draw for comfort. This apparent recoil inward from material chaos as if to seek some essential human or spiritual truth to set in opposition to it, has led to a general scholarly perception of Bellow as a neo-transcendentalist or humanist writer.

But to insist on the transcendental aspects of Bellow's work is to misrepresent him to a degree. One of the factors that make his fiction important as an account of the state of the West (and the state of the Western mind) after World War II is his constant engagement with the present moment; he looks closely at the cracks and fissures in contemporary society and at the workings of history that have led to them. Like Mr Sammler scrutinizing his planet he is aghast at what he discovers, and has to present a dissenting critique of it. This accounts for the lengthy essays or dissertations that punctuate his later fictions and have irritated many readers. But it is also a part of his great power as a novelist, which is the ability to present the urban experience, with an assurance that the material plurality of the world can be expressed and given meaning, and that 'civilization' is still possible. This is a moral stance, and although Bellow sees the complexity of the contemporary moment it is an essentially conservative stance (also authoritarian, since it depends upon a definition of civilization predicated on a particular set of interests).

It is a position that sets him counter to current fashions in fiction. During the early sixties (when Bellow was working on *Herzog*) a number of writers, most notably John Barth, Thomas Pynchon and Joseph Heller, began experimenting with the form and subject of the novel, creating a fiction now known as 'post-modernist'. Essentially, post-modernism proclaims the death of the novel, putting in its place a kind of anti-novel. It subverts the narrative order fundamental to realism, fragmenting the fictional form and, sometimes, the 'self' of the hero, who now is more likely to be an anti-hero. It is often metafictional, self-referential in its concern with the processes of fiction, like Barth's *The Sot-Weed Factor*. It may present its material as black comedy, dislocating its world into hilarious madness, like Heller's *Catch-22*, or into fantasy, like Kurt Vonnegut's *Slaughterhouse Five*.

Seen from the perspective of the post-modernists, Bellow is an unfashionable writer, denying all that their work implies. He remains stubbornly within his realist view of fiction, holding on to the past and to civilization. The sense of Bellow as a conservative figure is intensified by his association with such forecasters of the imminent triumph of barbarism as Allan Bloom. Yet, as Bellow clearly sees, a decline of literacy is a decline of culture, and even if we insist, with recent theoretical accounts, that there is no monolithic 'culture', but a plurality of cultures, the need to analyse and to understand is still paramount. As Bellow wrote in his foreword to Bloom's book, 'That poets – artists – should give new eyes to human beings, inducing them to view the world differently, converting them from fixed modes of experience, is ambition enough. ... What makes that project singularly difficult is the disheartening expansion of trained ignorance and bad thought'.[73] His alarm at the increasing spiritual devastation of the modern world, his fear of an encroaching anarchy, and his uncompromising insistence that there *are* better ways are well enough recorded in his novels. It may be that at times he lectures his readers, and his responses may sometimes seem little more than the complaints of a grouchy reactionary, out of tune with the age. In reality, he has much in common with Victor Wulpy in his story 'What Kind of Day Did You Have?', 'a mine of knowledge, a treasury of insights in all matters concerning the real needs and interests of modern human beings'. It is precisely his insistence on forcing us to look at what 'the age' means, his attempt to find, in history and in thought, something that is enduring, beyond the appeal of fashion and the current moment, that makes him valuable. The ambiguity that is characteristic of his endings is his acknowledgement that there are no easy answers, and his recasting, from novel to novel, of the difficult questions is something for which we should all be grateful.

Notes

1. Harold Bloom (ed.), *Saul Bellow: Modern Critical Views* (New York: Chelsea House Publishers, 1986), p. 1.
2. Saul Bellow (ed.), *Great Jewish Short Stories* (New York: Dell Publishing, 1963), p. 13.
3. Quoted in Stanley Kunitz (ed.) *Twentieth Century Authors*, First Supplement (New York: H.W. Wilson Company, 1955), p. 72.
4. Jo Brans, 'Common Needs, Common Preoccupations', in Stanley Trachtenberg (ed.) *Critical Essays on Saul Bellow* (Boston: G.K. Hall & Co., 1979), p. 67.
5. Saul Bellow, in his foreword to Allan Bloom, *The Closing of the American Mind* (New York: Simon and Schuster Inc., 1987), p.14.
6. Alfred Kazin, 'My Friend Saul Bellow', *Atlantic Monthly*, Jan. 1965, p. 51.
7. Mark Harris, *Saul Bellow: Drumlin Woodchuck* (Athens, GA: University of Georgia Press, 1980), p. 182.
8. Joyce Illig, 'An Interview with Saul Bellow', *Publishers Weekly*, 22 Oct. 1973, p. 77.
9. Saul Bellow, 'The Thinking Man's Waste Land', *Saturday Review*, 3 April 1965, p. 20.
10. Saul Bellow, *The Last Analysis* (London: Weidenfeld and Nicolson, 1966), p. vii.
11. Quoted in Mary Bruccoli (ed.), *Dictionary of Literary Biography, Documentary Series*, vol. 3 (Detroit: Gale Research Co., 1983), p. 62.
12. Joseph Epstein, 'A Talk with Saul Bellow', *New York Times Book Review*, 5 Dec. 1976, p. 3.
13. Noam Chomsky, 'Bellow's Israel', *New York Arts Journal*, Spring 1977, pp. 29–32.
14. Saul Bellow, 'I Haven't Hung up My Gloves Yet', *Toronto Star*, 11 March 1990, p. D6.
15. Saul Bellow, Foreword to Allan Bloom, *The Closing of the American Mind*, p. 13.
16. Brans, p. 66.
17. Harold Bloom, *Saul Bellow*, p. 1.
18. Gordon L. Harper, 'The Art of Fiction: Saul Bellow', *Paris Review*, 9 (1966), p. 56.
19. Edmund Wilson, *New Yorker*, 1 April 1944, p. 71; Delmore Schwartz, *Partisan Review*, 11 (1944), p. 348.

20. Bellow, *Great Jewish Short Stories*, p. 12.
21. Keith Opdahl, *The Novels of Saul Bellow*, (University Park, PA: Pennsylvania State University Press, 1967), p. 48; Robert Dutton, *Saul Bellow*, (Boston: Twayne Publishers, 1982), p. 19.
22. Alan S. Downer, *New York Times Book Review*, 30 Nov. 1947, p. 29.
23. Reuben Frank, 'Saul Bellow: The Evolution of a Contemporary Novelist', *Western Review*, 18 (1984), p. 108.
24. Joshua Trachtenberg, *The Devil and the Jews* (New York: Harper & Row, 1966), p. 3.
25. Clayton, p. 165.
26. Tony Tanner, *Saul Bellow* (Edinburgh: Oliver & Boyd, 1965) p. 36; Sarah Blacher Cohen, *Saul Bellow's Enigmatic Laughter* (Urbana: University of Illinois Press, 1974), p. 61.
27. Beatrice Kalb, 'Biographical Sketch', *Saturday Review of Literature*, (Sept. 1953), p. 13.
28. Harper, p. 56.
29. Harvey Breit, 'A Talk with Saul Bellow', *New York Times Book Review*, 20 Sept. 1953, p. 22.
30. Robert Penn Warren, 'The Man with No Commitments', *New Republic*, 2 Nov. 1953, p. 22; Norman Podhoretz, 'The Language of Life', *Commentary* 16 (1953), p. 80.
31. Opdahl, p. 74.
32. Warren, p. 23.
33. Leslie A. Fiedler, 'Saul Bellow', in Irving Malin (ed.) *Saul Bellow and the Critics* (New York: New York University Press, 1967), p. 7.
34. For a Freudian reading of the story see D. Weiss, 'Caliban on Prospero: A Psychoanalytic Study of the Novel *Seize the Day* by Saul Bellow', *American Imago* 19 (1962), pp. 227–306. For an account of Reich's influence see Eusebio Rodrigues, 'Reichianism in *Seize the Day*, in Stanley Trachtenberg, pp. 89–100.
35. Harvey Swados, 'A Breather from Saul Bellow', *New York Post Magazine*, 18 Nov. 1956, p. 11.
36. Robert O. Bowen, 'Bagels, Sour Cream and the Heart of the Current Novel', *Northwest Review*, 1 (1957), pp. 52–6; Fuchs, p. 83.
37. Saul Bellow, 'Deep Readers of the World, Beware', *New York Times Book Review*, 15 Feb. 1959, p. 1.
38. See Eusebio Rodrigues, *Quest for the Human: An Exploration of Saul Bellow's Fiction* (Lewisburg: Bucknell University Press, 1981), pp. 198–257.
39. Leslie Fiedler, *Waiting for the End* (Harmondsworth: Penguin Books, 1967), p. 109. See also Opdahl, pp. 124–6.
40. Tanner, p. 84.
41. Norman Podhoretz, *New York Herald Tribune Book Review*, 22 Feb. 1959, p. 3.
42. Fuchs, p. 99.
43. Bellow, *The Last Analysis*, p. vii.
44. Forest Read, '*Herzog*: A Review', *Epoch*, 14 (1964), p. 81.
45. David Galloway, *The Absurd Hero in American Fiction* (Austin: University of Texas Press, 1966), p. 138.

46. David Boroff, 'About the Author', *Saturday Review of Literature*, 19 Sept. 1964, p. 39.
47. Richard Poirier, 'Bellows to Herzog', *Partisan Review*, 32 (1965), p. 270.
48. J. W. Aldridge, 'The Complacency of *Herzog*', *Time to Murder and Create: The Contemporary Novel in Crisis* (New York: McKay, 1966), pp. 133–8.
49. Irving Howe, 'Odysseus, Flat on His Back', *New Republic*, 19 Sept. 1964, p. 26.
50. Brans, p. 66.
51. Keith Cushman, 'Mr. Bellow's *Sammler*: The Evolution of a Contemporary Text', in Stanley Trachtenberg, pp. 141–57.
52. Alfred Kazin, 'Though He Slay Me ...', *New York Review of Books*, 3 Dec. 1970, p. 3.
53. Harris, pp. 119–20.
54. Gerald Graff, *Literature Against Itself: Literary Ideas in Modern Society* (Chicago: University of Chicago Press, 1979), p. 230.
55. Brans, p. 58.
56. Richard Stern, 'Bellow's Gift', *The New York Times Magazine*, 21 Nov. 1976, pp. 46, 48.
57. Brans, p. 60.
58. Joseph Epstein, 'A Talk with Saul Bellow', *New York Times Book Review*, 5 Dec. 1976, p. 93.
59. Quoted in 'A Laureate Blinks in the Limelight', *New York Times*, 22 Oct. 1976, p. 10.
60. Harold Bloom, *Saul Bellow*, p. 5.
61. Saul Bellow, *To Jerusalem and Back: A Personal Account* (Harmondsworth: Penguin Books, 1977), p. 164.
62. William Kennedy, 'If Saul Bellow Doesn't Have a True Word to Say, He Keeps His Mouth Shut', *Esquire*, Feb. 1982, p. 50.
63. Fuchs, pp. 305–9; Jonathan Wilson, *On Bellow's Planet: Readings from the Dark Side* (Cranbury NJ: Fairleigh Dickenson University Press, 1985), p. 29.
64. Terrence Rafferty, 'Hearts and Minds', *New Yorker*, 20 July 1987, pp. 89–91.
65. Stephen L. Tanner, 'The Religious Vision of *More Die of Heartbreak*', in Gloria L. Cronin and L. H. Goldman, *Saul Bellow in the 1980s: A Collection of Critical Essays* (Urbana: University of Illinois Press, 1988), pp. 283–96.
66. See reviews by Charles Michaud, *Library Journal*, 15 March 1989, p. 84; William H. Pritchard, *Hudson Review*, Autumn, 1989, p. 490; John Updike, *New Yorker*, 1 May 1989, pp. 111, 113–14.
67. Robert Towers, *New York Review of Books*, 7 April 1989, p. 50.
68. In a letter to the author, 25 Oct. 1989.
69. Unsigned review, *New Yorker*, 23 Oct. 1989, p. 146.
70. Irving Malin (ed.), *Saul Bellow and the Critics* (Carbondale: Southern Illinois University Press, 1967), p. vii.
71. Harold Bloom, *The Anxiety of Influence: A Theory of Poetry* (New York and London: Oxford University Press, 1973).

72. Saul Bellow, 'Starting Out in Chicago', *American Scholar*, 44 (Winter 1974–5), p. 72.
73. Saul Bellow, Foreword to Allan Bloom, *The Closing of the American Mind*, p. 17.

Select Bibliography

BELLOW'S PRINCIPAL WRITINGS

Dangling Man (1944)
The Victim (1947)
The Adventures of Augie March (1953)
Seize the Day (1956)
Henderson the Rain King (1959)
Herzog (1964)
The Last Analysis (1965)
Mosby's Memoirs and Other Stories (1968)
Mr. Sammler's Planet (1970)
Humboldt's Gift (1975)
To Jerusalem and Back: A Personal Account (1976)
The Dean's December (1982)
Him with His Foot in His Mouth and Other Stories (1984)
More Die of Heartbreak (1987)
The Theft (1989)
The Bellarosa Connection (1989)

SELECTED CRITICISM

Bloom, Harold (ed.), *Saul Bellow: Modern Critical Views* (New York: Chelsea House Publishers, 1986).
——, *Saul Bellow's Herzog* (New York: Chelsea House Publishers, 1988).
Bradbury, Malcolm, *Saul Bellow* (London: Methuen, 1982).
Braham, Jeanne A., *A Sort of Columbus: The American Voyages of Saul Bellow* (Athens: University of Georgia Press, 1984).
Clayton, John J., *Saul Bellow: In Defense of Man* (Bloomington, University of Indiana Press, 1979).
Cohen, Sarah Blacher, *Saul Bellow's Enigmatic Laughter* (Urbana, University of Illinois Press, 1974).
Cronin, Gloria L. and L. H. Goldman, *Saul Bellow in the 1980s: A Collection of Critical Essays* (East Lansing: Michigan State University Press, 1989).
Dutton, Robert, *Saul Bellow* (Boston: Twayne Publishers, 1982).
Fuchs, Daniel, *Saul Bellow: Vision and Revision* (Durham N.C.: Duke University Press, 1984).

Goldman, Liela H., *Saul Bellow's Moral Vision: A Study of the Jewish Experience* (New York: Irvington Publishers, 1983).

Kiernan, Robert F., *Saul Bellow* (New York: Continuum, 1989).

McCadden, Joseph F., *The Flight from Women in the Fiction of Saul Bellow* (Lanham, MD: University Press of America, 1980).

Malin, Irving (ed.), *Saul Bellow and the Critics* (New York: New York University Press, 1967).

——, *Saul Bellow's Fiction* (Carbondale: Southern Illinois University Press, 1969).

Newman, Judie, *Saul Bellow and History* (London: Macmillan Press, 1984).

Opdahl, Keith, *The Novels of Saul Bellow* (University Park, PA: Pennsylvania State University Press, 1967).

Pifer, Ellen, *Saul Bellow: Against the Grain* (Philadelphia: University of Pennsylvania Press, 1990).

Porter, M. Gilbert, *Whence the Power? The Artistry and Humanity of Saul Bellow* (Columbia: University of Missouri Press, 1974).

Rodrigues, Eusebio L., *Quest for the Human: An Exploration of Saul Bellow's Fiction* (Lewisburg, PA: Bucknell University Press, 1981).

Tanner, Tony, *Saul Bellow* (Edinburgh: Oliver and Boyd, 1965).

Trachtenberg, Stanley (ed.), *Critical Essays on Saul Bellow* (Boston: G. K. Hall, 1979).

Wilson, Jonathan, *On Bellow's Planet: Readings from the Dark Side* (Cranbury, NJ: Fairleigh Dickinson University Press, 1985).

There is now a variety of bibliographies of Bellow's works and critical writings on them. Currently, the most comprehensive and up-to-date is Gloria L. Cronin and Blaine H. Hall (eds), *Saul Bellow: An Annotated Bibliography*, Second Edition (New York & London: Garland Publishing, Inc., 1987).

Index

813.52   Hyland, Peter
BELLOW   Saul Bellow.
HYLAND, PETER
SAUL BELLOW
                    29.95

$29.95

DATE			

B86   j44

a8